# Beyond
# Traditional Phonics

# Beyond Traditional Phonics

## RESEARCH DISCOVERIES AND READING INSTRUCTION

### Margaret Moustafa
California State University
at Los Angeles

HEINEMANN
PORTSMOUTH, NH

**Heinemann**
A division of Reed Elsevier Inc.
361 Hanover Street
Portsmouth, NH 03801-3912

*Offices and agents throughout the world*

**Library of Congress Cataloging-in-Publication Data**

Moustafa, Margaret.
    Beyond traditional phonics : research discoveries and reading
  instruction / Margaret Moustafa.
        p.    cm.
    Includes bibliographical references and index.
    ISBN 0-435-07247-1 (alk. paper)
    1. Reading—Phonetic method.  2. Language experience approach in education.  3. Reading.  I. Title.
  LB1050.34.M68   1997
  372.46'5—dc21                                                97-22907
                                                                   CIP

Editor: Lois Bridges
Production: Melissa L. Inglis
Cover design: Darci Mehall/Aureo Design
Manufacturing: Louise Richardson

Cover photo © Digital Stock

Printed in the United States of America on acid-free paper
01 00 99 98    DA        4 5 6 7 8 9

To children,
in support of their efforts
to read

and to those
who support them

# Contents

# 7

# How Children Use Their Knowledge About Reading to Read    71

# 8

# Beyond Traditional Phonics    85

# List of Figures

# Acknowledgments

I wish to thank the many researchers I cite in this book. I would also like to thank Lois Bridges, Mary Maxwell, Connie Weaver, and Sandra Wilde for their encouragement and constructive criticism of various drafts of the book; Patricia Clancy, David Eskey, Shirley Brice Heath, Michael Kamil, Stephen Krashen, Stephen Kucer, Reynaldo Macias, Elba Maldonado-Colon, and Frank Manis for their contributions to my research; Dirk and Ruth Heiss for inspiring my work; and Mohamed, Shereef, and Tamir Moustafa and Fred Heiss for their emotional and technical support.

# Introduction

WE ARE IN A GROAN ZONE—A TRANSITIONAL TIME WHEN OUR two-millennium-old cultural beliefs about how children learn to read are being broadened and challenged by surprising, counterintuitive research findings. These findings originated in the 1960s when research in reading looked beyond the "visible," or print, system involved in learning to read and began investigating the "invisible," or linguistic, cognitive, and social systems involved in learning to read.

I call this transitional period the groan zone because, even as researchers are learning more and more about the invisible systems involved in learning to read and a growing minority of teachers are using this knowledge to inform instruction, this knowledge has not yet become part of our general cultural knowledge. And, as inevitably happens when deeply rooted, traditional belief systems are challenged by new knowledge, the backlash has begun. Concerned parents, policy makers, journalists, and legislators, aware of the visible system involved in learning to read and not yet aware of the invisible systems, are calling for a return to phonics instruction—instruction in letter-sound correspondences—as a route into reading because that is how they believe children learn to read.

Published in 1990, Marilyn Adams's book *Beginning to Read* supports the traditional view of how children learn to read. Commissioned by Congress "to provide guidance as to how schools might maximize the quality of phonic instruction in beginning reading programs" (p. 29), *Beginning to Read* summarizes a large body of correlational research on the visible system. This research has been interpreted to support the view that phonics knowledge is a necessary prerequisite to learning to read. Although this view is not new—

indeed, as we shall see, it is quite old—*Beginning to Read* is perhaps the most widely quoted book of the decade on how children learn to read. Often when we encounter a reference to "the research" on reading, it means the research embodied in Adams's book.

While the research summarized in *Beginning to Read* is extensive, it is also selective. Because Adams was commissioned by Congress to report on the visible system involved in learning to read, she ignored much of the groundbreaking research on the role of the invisible systems. Additionally, at the time the book was written, some fundamental discoveries about how children learn letter-sound correspondences had yet to be made or understood.

Since the 1960s researchers and educators have learned a great deal about reading and how children learn to read. We recognize that there is much more to learning to read than just learning sounds associated with letters. We understand more about the abilities children have that enable them to read and we now know how to build on children's strengths (rather than their weaknesses) to help them become proficient readers. We also understand the kind of support children need from us in order to learn to read. But most important, we have abandoned our traditional assumption that reading is pronouncing written words, and have moved on to a new definition of reading as one of making sense of written messages.

> Learning to read should be a joyous adventure, as exciting for youngsters, their families, and their teachers as when children learn to walk and talk. The key to making the journey a happy one is that we provide appropriate support.

This book summarizes some of the important research not included in Adams's book. It also provides an update on the amazing discoveries about how children learn letter-sound correspondences, discoveries that have been made since Adams wrote *Beginning to Read*. Finally, it presents a method of teaching phonics that is remarkably like, yet radically different from, traditional phonics instruction. It is a method of teaching phonics that may enable us to move beyond today's groan zone into a new consensus on how best to help children learn to read.

Learning to read doesn't have to be hard and frustrating. It can and should be a joyous adventure, as exciting for youngsters, their families, and their teachers as when children learn to walk and talk. The key to making the journey a happy and successful one is that we, who already know how to read, understand how children learn to read and provide them with appropriate support and encouragement.

Whether you work with children at home or at school, whether you are involved as a policy maker, journalist, community leader, or concerned citizen, there will be surprises in this book for you. There will also be concrete suggestions throughout the book on how to appropriately support children's efforts to become readers.

I begin this account of how children learn to read by describing in Chapter 1 what we have traditionally believed about learning to read. I do this because many of the popularly held assumptions about learning to read are deeply rooted in our culture, originating long before modern research on reading.

Chapter 2 examines some of the problems recent research has uncovered that challenge our traditional assumptions about how children learn the letter-sound system. As you will see in the later chapters, children do not begin their journey into literacy learning about the letter-sound system. However, it is the place where most literate adults begin when they think about teaching children to read. Therefore, I begin where most people begin.

Chapter 3 presents the amazing, counterintuitive discoveries about linguistic processes children use to figure out unfamiliar print words. These discoveries, more than any others, have plunged us into the groan zone.

Chapter 4 explains some of the misunderstandings that have occurred because some people know about the discoveries described in Chapter 3, while others have yet to learn about them.

Chapter 5 describes some exciting new discoveries that reveal how children learn letter-sound correspondences. I believe that once these discoveries and their implications for reading instruction are understood, we will move beyond today's groan zone into a new public consensus.

Chapter 6 describes cognitive and social processes that enable children to make sense of print. It explains schema theory and the role of background knowledge in making sense of print.

Chapter 7 describes how children begin their journey into literacy. This chapter describes the profound effect being read to—or not being read to—and having access to age-appropriate books—or not having access to age-appropriate books—have on children's literacy development.

Then, Chapter 8 describes a new method of teaching phonics. This method aids and supports children's journey into literacy far better than traditional phonics instruction and may allow the diverse voices in literacy education to come together in a new consensus on how to best to teach reading. But don't skip to the end to read it. You won't fully understand Chapter 8 unless you are familiar with the information in Chapters 1 through 7.

Finally, in the Epilogue, I offer some suggestions on where we go from here and make some recommendations for public policy.

Educators, psychologists, linguists, and sociolinguists have discovered most of the information in this book in the last forty years. In this account of how children learn to read, I avoid as much as possible (except to illustrate a point) research conducted on skilled, adult readers and focus, instead, on research done on children learning to read. I do this because what is true for literate adults may not necessarily be true for children learning to read. Furthermore, what one does as a proficient reader may not necessarily be the same as what a new, inexperienced reader does.

In the following pages I distinguish words that are written from words that are spoken. I do this by referring to words that are written as *print words* or *written words* and words that are spoken as *spoken words*. In using the terms *print words* and *written words* I do not mean to refer to a particular style of script.

I also distinguish words that are written from words that are spoken by italicizing print words and writing the sounds of spoken words between slashes. Thus, *cat* represents a print word and /kat/ represents its spoken form.

Finally, I use the terms *pronounce print words* and *convert print words into spoken language* interchangeably without reference to any one type of accent such as a midwestern, Boston, southern, or Australian accent. (We all speak with one accent or another.) The dialect the reader uses in his or her day-to-day spoken communication is the correct dialect for him or her to use when making sense of print.

Regrettably a body of research I do not report in this book addresses how children learn to write. Reading and writing are intimately related. Discussing reading without writing tells only half of the story. Just as we are making surprising, counterintuitive discoveries about how children learn to read, so we are making surprising, counterintuitive discoveries about how children learn to write. However, to provide timely information on our new knowledge about how children learn to read, I must limit this book to reading.

Let us begin.

# 1

# Our Traditional Assumptions About How Children Learn to Read

IN THE LAST FOUR DECADES OUR UNDERSTANDING OF HOW children learn to read has undergone monumental change. The change is as fundamental as the realization that the world is round or that the earth revolves around the sun—and just as counterintuitive. These new understandings have profound implications for how we help children learn to read. They can make the difference between a child struggling—and perhaps failing—to learn to read and the same child succeeding and delighting in learning to read.

The purpose of this book is to inform you of the exciting discoveries we have made about how children learn to read and how you can help them become competent readers. Yet to begin in the 1960s, when our understandings of reading began to change, is to tell the story without setting the scene. Hence, I begin with a short overview of the origins of our traditional assumptions about how children learn to read and some of the problems we have discovered about these assumptions. I then explain our new understandings and how they can help children learn to read.

## In the Beginning

The assumption that children learn to read by being taught letters is deeply rooted in our culture. It is probably as old as alphabetic writing itself. In ancient Greece, Plato quoted Socrates as saying the following:

In learning to read . . . we were satisfied when we knew the letters of the alphabet . . . everywhere eager to make them out; and not thinking of ourselves perfect in the art of reading until we recognize them wherever they are found. (*The Republic*, III, 402A. Cited in Venezky 1967)

Instruction based on this assumption is just as old. In the first century A.D., a Roman educator, Quintilian, used tablets with letters on them to teach children to read (Smith 1965).

> The assumption that children learn to read by being taught letters is probably as old as alphabetic writing itself.

Perhaps the first challenge to the assumption that children learn to read by learning letters or letter-sound correspondences began about two centuries ago. In the late 1700s a German educator, Frederick Gedike, argued that children should be taught whole words rather than parts of words. He pointed out that words are meaningful, whereas letters, in and of themselves, are not. Gedike maintained:

> It is neither necessary nor useful to begin learning to read with a knowledge of the individual letters, but it is not only far more pleasant but also far more useful for the child if it learns to read entire words at once, because in this way it will be occupied immediately with whole ideas, but on the contrary the ABC's and spelling supply the child with only fragments of ideas. (Cited in Balmuth 1982)

At least since that time,[1] educators and parents alike have argued over the relative merits of the various *letter-emphasis* and *word-emphasis* approaches. The letter-emphasis approach, which teaches letter-phoneme correspondences, became known as the *phonics approach* and the word-emphasis approach, which teaches whole words, became known as the *whole word approach*.

---

[1]The idea that children should be taught whole words rather than the sounds of letters may predate Gedike. Emund Burke Huey (1908–1968) attributed the original suggestion for the Language Experience Approach (in which the teacher writes down what the children say and then teaches them to read what they said) to John Amos Comenius (1592–1670).

The first theoretical research on reading was conducted a century after Gedike argued for a whole word approach. In 1886, James Cattell, an American in Germany, reported on two experiments with adult subjects. In one experiment, he found it takes readers twice as long to name random letters as it takes them to name a meaningful word with the same number of letters. Here is an illustration of what Cattell found. Look at the following two lines and see which one you identify faster:

Mary

ymrg

Did you identify the first line faster than the second?

In the other experiment Cattell found that it takes readers twice as long to name three or four random words as it takes them to name a sentence with the same number of words. Here is another illustration. Look at the following two lines and see which one you identify faster:

Let me show you

you me show let.

Again, did you identify the first line faster than the second?

Unfortunately, as we shall see in Chapter 3, Cattell's finding that sentences can be identified faster than random words was largely ignored by practitioners at the time. However, his finding that whole words can be identified faster than letters, a finding that was compatible with Gedike's argument a century before, was used to support the whole word approach to reading instruction.

Cattell's research on reading inspired other research on reading. Some of the research supported the phonics approach and some supported the whole word approach (Venezky 1977).

The argument continued. Those who thought children learn to read by learning the sounds of letters advocated beginning reading materials where the text was controlled to use letter-phoneme correspondences that had been taught. Those who thought children learn to read by learning to recognize whole print words advocated beginning reading materials where the text was controlled to use words that had been taught.

At the beginning of this century *McGuffey's Eclectic Primer* combined the letter-emphasis and word-emphasis approaches. In the preface to the 1909 edition the publishers wrote, "The plan of the book enables the teacher to pursue the Phonic Method, the Word Method, the Alphabetic Method, or any combination of these methods" (1909, p. iii). The first book in the series began with two alphabet charts, one with uppercase letters and one with lowercase letters. Then, with illustrations of a cat and a rat, Lesson 1 went as follows:

> a and cat rat
> a c d n r t
> a rat     a cat
> A cat           A rat
> A cat and a rat.
> A rat and a cat.

Lesson 2 on the following page was

> at the ran has
> Ann
> h th s
> The cat    the rat
> The cat has a rat.
> The rat ran at Ann.
> Ann has a cat.
> The cat ran at the rat.

Gradually, through the efforts of educators such as Horace Mann, the whole word approach became more widely used in U.S. schools. By the 1930s and 1940s, most publishers of beginning reading instructional programs for children designed programs that taught children to read whole words and deemphasized letter-phoneme, or phonics, instruction (Chall 1967). Edward Dolch published a list of the 220 most common print words (e.g., *a, about, after, again, all, always, am, an, and, any, are, around, as, ask, at*, etc.) and urged teachers to teach these words as "sight words" to struggling readers (Dolch 1945). Millions of children were taught to read short, multipage "stories" bound with other "stories" into a reading textbook, or basal, such as the following:

> See Sally work.
> Work, work, work.
> Sally can work.
> See Sally work.
> Oh, Dick.
> Oh, Jane.
> See, see.

Sally can work.
Oh, Sally.
Funny, funny Sally.
Oh, oh, oh.
(*The New Basic Readers*, 1956, pp. 7–10)

In these stories the story line was in the pictures, not the print. Readers had to look at the picture to understand the story. (The pictures in the story above show Sally "cleaning" her room by hiding her toys under her bed and Dick and Jane discovering the toys under the bed. Would you have known it from reading the text?)

Then, in 1955, in his book *Why Johnny Can't Read*, Rudolph Flesch blamed illiteracy on a lack of phonics instruction in schools. He later showed unfamiliar print words such as *inert* and *stoic* to first- and second-grade children in a phonics program, and the children "read and pronounced [the words] without trouble" (Flesch 1979). He implored parents to make sure their children were taught the sounds of letters so they would learn how to read. His appeal touched a chord with parents. Many Americans began to question the trend away from letter-emphasis, or phonics, instruction.

Publishers of children's reading textbooks once again produced reading programs where both the sounds of letters and whole words were taught (Durkin 1987). Only this time, phonics was taught through workbook exercises and the children's readers continued to be organized largely around whole word principles. Those who did poorly in the readers were given heavier doses of phonics instruction at the expense of time spent reading stories (Allington 1983; Hiebert 1983). This was the dominant method of instruction in U.S. schools when today's generation of parents, journalists, and policy makers attended elementary school.

Although they differ, both the phonics approach and the whole word approach, each born in the preresearch era, actually share a basic assumption: they both assume that learning to read is a parts-to-whole process. As children learn the parts of reading—letters or words—they will understand the whole. Both, unaware that readers unconsciously use their knowledge of the language represented in the text to read, produce texts that use distorted rather than natural language. Where but in a child's reader would one find sentences such as "The cat has a rat. The rat ran at Ann" and "Oh, Dick. Oh, Jane. See, see. Sally can work."? As we will see in Chapter 3, this well-intended attempt to make learning to read easier for children actually makes it more difficult.

Until this century, both the phonics approach and the whole word approach shared another assumption: if one is converting print into spoken language, one is reading. This began to change when, in order to test large groups of army recruits in World War I, we began giving silent reading tests with comprehension questions. The tests showed that, despite having been taught to read in school, many adults could not comprehend materials at the level of a daily newspaper (Resnick and Resnick 1977).

As we became aware that pronouncing print is not necessarily comprehending print, comprehension was added to reading instruction. First children were taught to say print words. Later they were taught "reading comprehension." The unit of comprehension was viewed as the word. We thought that if children understood each word, they would understand the message. As we shall see later in this book, this is not necessarily true.

## A New Dawn

In the 1960s a fundamental change in our thinking about how children learn to read occurred when Noam Chomsky, Roger Brown, and others pointed out that children learn much more than what they are intentionally taught. Psychologists, linguists, and educators began to refer to children as active learners who contribute to their own learning. Within the next three decades, under the influence of cognitive psychology, we were swept up in a cascade of new understandings about reading and how children learn to read.

| |
|---|
| Reading is making sense of print. |

Reading theorists rejected the traditional conception of reading as pronouncing words and redefined it as a process of making sense of print. That is, if children are pronouncing *inert* or *stoic* but they don't understand what they are "reading," they are not reading. In a similar way, you may pick up a book or a newspaper in Portuguese, for example, and say the words but not comprehend the message. That, according to the new definition of reading, is *not* reading. Reading occurs only if comprehension occurs.

Reading theorists also reconceptualized how readers make sense of print. As we shall see in Chapter 3, Kenneth Goodman and others demonstrated that children use their knowledge of spoken language as well as their knowledge of the letter-sound system to read. Others demonstrated that readers also use their background knowledge to make sense of print. A consensus arose among reading theorists that readers use their knowledge of the language represented in the text, their background knowledge, and their knowledge of the letter-sound system to make sense of alphabetic writing. This new view of the reading process is called the *transactional model* of reading. It is the view of the reading process that I present in this book.

As the research evidence was growing for the transactional model of reading, some startling discoveries were being made about our traditional assumptions regarding letter-sound correspondences in English and how children learn them. These discoveries raised questions about the efficacy of traditional letter-sound, or phonics, instruction. I will examine these discoveries in the next chapter. Then, in the following chapters, I will describe exciting recent discoveries that have been made about how children figure out unfamiliar print words.

# 2

# Problems with Our Traditional Assumptions About How Children Learn Letter-Sound Correspondences

## *Traditional Phonics Generalizations*

Perhaps the first surprise about phonics instruction was Theodore Clymer's discovery in the 1960s that traditional phonics generalizations are not all that reliable. Clymer (1963) looked at four popular reading programs for children and chose forty-five of the most clearly stated phonics generalizations in these programs. He then compared these phonics generalizations with the words used in the stories in these reading programs.

One of the generalizations Clymer examined was the popular silent *e* generalization: "When there are two vowels, one of which is a final *e*, the first vowel is long and the *e* is silent" (or, as some versions put it, "the first vowel says its name"). Clymer found the silent *e* generalization works with words such as *bone, came, date,* and *time* but not with words such as *done, come, have,* and *were*. In fact, Clymer found the silent *e* generalization worked in only 63 percent of the words to which the generalization could be applied in the four reading programs he inspected.

This wasn't the only surprise. Of over thirty vowel generalizations Clymer tested, only half of them worked at least 60 percent of the time.

What if we were to teach just the generalizations that work? The problem, Clymer found, is that the most reliable generalizations often apply to infrequent letter-sound patterns. For example, one of the few generalizations that Clymer found worked 100 percent of the time in the 2,600 words he examined was "When a word begins with *kn*, the *k* is silent." Yet, if you have not skipped anything so far in this book, you have encountered only five words with an initial *kn*: know, knows, known, knowledge, and knew, hardly enough to justify teaching the generalization.

Others must have been surprised by Clymer's findings. While researchers seldom set out to do replication studies, at least three researchers—Mildred Bailey (1967), Lou Burmeister (1968), and Robert Emans (1967)—did replication studies of Clymer's work. In each case the results were similar.

Perhaps the problem was that the phonics generalizations were written poorly and they just needed to be written better. Betty Berdiansky, Bruce Cronnell, and John Koehler (1969), building on the work of Richard Venezky (1967), approached the problem from another direction. Rather than looking at the phonics generalizations and testing them against print words, they began with print words and analyzed them to develop better generalizations. They analyzed over six thousand one- and two-syllable print words within the comprehension vocabularies of children ages six to nine years old.

In their analysis Berdiansky's group made an assumption—one shared by all scholars up to that time—that the unit of sound represented in alphabetic script is what is known as the *phoneme* (pronounced /fo.nem/). Phonemes are small units of sounds in spoken words. They are often represented by one letter such as *c*, *k*, *u*, or *e* but sometimes they are represented by pairs of letters, called *digraphs*, such as *ck* or *ue*. The word *black*, for example, has five letters which represent four phonemes: /b/, /l/, /a/, and /k/.

First, Berdiansky's group listed all the single letters (such as *c* and *k*) and digraphs (such as *ck* and *ue*) that represent a phoneme. Then, they looked for letter-phoneme correspondences such as the letter *c* is pronounced /k/ or /s/; the digraph *ck* is pronounced /k/.

Again the findings were startling. Among the one- and two-syllable words Berdiansky and her associates examined, they found sixty-nine letters and digraphs used to represent thirty-eight phonemes. A manageable number you might say. But here's the catch—the sixty-nine letters and digraphs were related to the thirty-eight phonemes in 211 different ways!

To illustrate the complexity they found, let's look at just some of the ways the letter *o* is pronounced. In my midwestern dialect, *o* is pronounced one way in *no*, another way in *to*, another way in *won*, and yet another way in *woman*. The letters *ow* are pronounced one way in *now* and another way in *snow* (which, incidentally, is the same as the *o* in *no*). The letters *oe* are pronounced one way in *shoe*, another way in *does* (when *does* is a verb, not a noun), and yet another way in *doe* (which is the same as the *o* in *no* and the *ow* in *snow*).

Looked at another way, the vowels in *know* and *now* are written the same but pronounced differently, while the vowels in *no* and *know* are written differently but pronounced the same.

Berdiansky's group found that even the consonants, which we have traditionally assumed are more "regular" than vowels, are not all that regular. For example, *s* is pronounced one way in *books* and another way in *dogs*; *c* is pronounced one way in *carrot* and another way in *celery* (which is the same as the *s* in *books*); *g* is pronounced one way in *get* and another way in *gem* (even though both are at the beginning of the word and both are followed by the letter *e*); *f* is pronounced one way in *often* and another way in *of*; *ph* is pronounced one way in *shepherd* and another way in *telephone* (which is the same as the *f* in *often*).

In short, Berdiansky's group found that letter-phoneme correspondences are not just a handful or two of letter-phoneme correspondences or even a manageable group of seventy or so letter-phoneme correspondences as some suggest. Rather they are a complex, mind-boggling web of correspondences.

> Letter-phoneme correspondences are a complex, mind-boggling web of correspondences.

Berdiansky's group also counted the number of words to which each letter-phoneme correspondence applied and called those correspondences that applied to at least ten different print words "generalizations." Among the 211 letter-phoneme correspondences Berdiansky's group found, there were 166 letter-phoneme generalizations—106 for vowels and sixty for consonants. We can only wonder how many more generalizations Berdiansky and her associates would have found if they had also analyzed words of three or more syllables—or if they had accounted for different accents readers have (e.g., a New York, Boston, or southern accent).

The implications of this discovery are staggering. Those of us who have tried (and tried and tried) to teach young children generalizations such as, "Look both ways before you cross the street," "Wash your hands before you eat," and "Don't talk with your mouth full" can appreciate the enormity of the task of helping children remember and apply more than 166 letter-phoneme generalizations. If a reading program taught one generalization a week (with no time allowances for review, testing, and reteaching), nine months a year, every year, for four years, kindergarten through third grade, it would cover only 144 generalizations.

But more important, even if a child were to learn all 166 generalizations for one- and two-syllable words, how would he or she know which one to use when he or she encountered a letter or digraph with multiple possible pronunciations? Should the *o* in *do* be pronounced /o/ or /oo/ or /u/? (That is, like the *o* in *no*, or like the *o* in *to*, or like the *o* in *won*?) To say that a word is "regular" (that it fits the generalizations) or "irregular" (that it doesn't fit the generalizations) is no help to a child encountering an unfamiliar print word. How is a child to know if a print word is regular or irregular until after he or she knows what the word is?

Worse yet, when Cronnell reversed the 166 letter-phoneme generalizations Berdiansky, Cronnell, and Koehler developed for readers, less than half of the 166 generalizations worked for spellers (Adams 1990, p. 389).

## *Children's Perceptions of Sounds in Spoken Words*

While Clymer, Berdiansky and her associates, and other researchers were discovering the complexity of the letter-sound system and its implications for traditional phonics instruction, another group of researchers was pursuing a different line of investigation. Rather than looking at the letter-phoneme rules, they looked at children themselves and their perception of phonemes. (Remember that phonemes are small units of sounds in spoken words that are represented by single letters such as *c*, *k*, *u*, or *e*, or pairs of letters, called digraphs, such as *ck* or *ue*.)

In this line of research, the first surprise came when D. J. Bruce (1964) demonstrated that young children have difficulty manipulating phonemes. Bruce gave young children words and asked them to make other words by deleting phonemes. For example, he said *fork* and asked the children to say it without the /k/; he said *snail* and asked the children to say it without the /n/. (The children were expected to respond with *for* and *sail*.)

None of the five- and six-year-old children was able to do the task with any of the words Bruce tried. The seven-year-olds averaged only two correct answers out of the thirty words. Only the eight- and nine-year-olds had any success. On the average, the eight-year-olds got about 50 percent of the words right and the nine-year-olds got almost all the words right.

Perhaps the problem was that the children didn't understand the task. Perhaps Bruce's task, which became known as the phoneme deletion task, required some teaching first. Jerome Rosner (1974) set out to demonstrate that with instruction children could learn to do the phoneme deletion task. He taught it to kindergartners for a whole school year and still found similar, disappointing results.

Perhaps the phoneme deletion task was too difficult. Perhaps it didn't represent what children do when they learn to read. So Isabelle Liberman, Donald Shankweiler, F. William Fischer, and Bonnie Carter (1974) tried it yet another way. They gave children a much simpler task. All the children had to do was tap out the number of phonemes in a spoken word. For example, with the spoken word *big*, a child was expected to tap three times, one time for /b/, one time for /i/, and one time for /g/. This task became known as the phoneme tapping task.

Once again the results were surprising. Liberman and her associates found that 83 percent of the kindergartners they tested could not analyze spoken words into phonemes most of the time. That is, they usually could not abstract spoken sounds into units represented by single letters and digraphs before systematic instruction in reading began. They even found that 30 percent of the children they tested at the end of first grade could not analyze spoken words into phonemic segments most of the time.

---

Instruction in letter-phoneme correspondences doesn't make sense to children who have not yet learned to read.

---

Again replication studies were done. Linnea Ehri and Lee Wilce (1980), Virginia Mann (1986), Rebecca Treiman and Jonathan Baron (1981), and William Tunmer and Andrew Nesdale (1985)—to name just a few—all did similar studies and all found similar results.

The inescapable conclusion from this line of research is that children don't analyze speech into phonemes before they begin to read the way we literate adults have traditionally thought they do. If children have difficulty analyzing spoken words into phonemes, how can they understand instruction in letter-phoneme correspondences?

Something was wrong with our traditional assumptions about how children acquire letter-sound correspondences. Instruction in letter-phoneme correspondences may feel right to literate adults who can make sense of it. However, it doesn't make sense to children who have not yet learned to read.

How then do children learn to read? That—with the exception of Chapter 4—is what the remainder of this book is about.

# 3

# How Children Use Language to Figure Out Unfamiliar Print Words

## *Alphabetic Writing and Holistic Reading*

If reading is making sense of print, it is not necessary to "sound out" print words in order to read them. The first writing systems mankind developed were *logographic*. In logographic writing systems, logos, or symbols, stand for concepts.

Logos are used worldwide on public signs such as a silhouette of a skirted person on a door in a public building, a picture of a cigarette in a circle with a line drawn through it, or a curved line with an arrow at a street intersection. When we use computers, we click on icons, or logos.

The best-known logographic writing system for longer, more expressive messages is the traditional Chinese writing system. In logographic writing systems each print word has a separate symbol, or character, and children are taught each character, one by one. In China children are required to memorize 3,100 characters in elementary school and 4,000 to 5,000 characters in secondary school (Jiang and Li 1985).

In an alphabetic writing system the sounds of words are represented rather than the concepts. Although the English writing system is predominately alphabetic, it also includes some logographic writing. For example, read the following sentence:

Mr. Smith paid $12.

In this sentence, the words *Smith* and *paid* are written alphabetically. The symbols represent the pronunciations of the spoken words. In the same sentence, *Mr.*, *$*, and *12* are written logographically. The symbols do not represent the pronunciations of spoken words; rather, they represent concepts. (Although *Mr.* happens to be written with letters, the letters do not represent its pronunciation.) Readers learn to recognize these symbols holistically, as in the traditional Chinese writing system.

Each system has its advantages. An advantage of a logographic system is that people who speak different languages can read it. Speakers of Spanish, French, German, and English can all make sense of the logo (or numeral) 12.

An advantage of an alphabetic writing system is that once children learn letter-sound correspondences, they do not have to be taught each word, one by one. Rather they can use their knowledge of the letter-sound system to figure out how to say print words they have never seen before without help from another reader. That is, they can figure out how to convert unfamiliar print words into spoken language by themselves.

> # Readers learn to recognize print words holistically.

Although logographic and alphabetic print are written differently, they are not necessarily read differently. That is, just because a word is written alphabetically, it doesn't have to be read alphabetically, letter by letter. Readers can learn to recognize print words holistically, whether they are written alphabetically or logographically.[1] In cultures where an alphabetic system is used, the first print words preschool children learn to recognize—such as their names, STOP on stop signs, and commercial names such as McDonald's—are read holistically.[2] In kindergartens in the United States, children are typically taught to read color words such as *red*, *blue*, and *green* and the names of their classmates holistically without analyzing their parts. The whole word method of teaching reading makes use of children's ability to recognize whole print words. In short, alphabetic writing can be read both alphabetically and holistically.

---

[1]This was the point in the word perception studies done on skilled, adult readers at the end of the last century (Cattell 1886; Pillsbury 1897; Erdmann and Dodge 1898) and extended and refined by researchers in the 1960s and 1970s (Tulving and Gold 1963; Reicher 1969; and Schuberth and Eimas 1977).

[2]Goodman (1986); Goodman and Goodman (1979); Harste, Burke, and Woodward (1982). Also see Kimura and Bryant's (1983) study of seven-year-old children applying logographic reading strategies to alphabetic script as well as Ehri and Wilce's (1985) study.

Similarly, even though a print word has been initially identified through letter-sound correspondences, it doesn't always have to be identified that way on subsequent encounters. Once it becomes familiar, it can be identified holistically. That is why you probably were not even aware when you were reading *Mr. Smith paid $12* that *Smith* and *paid* are written alphabetically but *Mr.*, *$*, and *12* are written logographically. You probably read all the words holistically.

## Another Way of Figuring Out Unfamiliar Print Words

In 1965, through an ingenious experiment, Kenneth Goodman showed that children have another way, besides letter-sound correspondences or being told by another reader, to learn how to pronounce unfamiliar print words. In the experiment, words were taken from stories in children's readers and put in lists. (The stories had not been used at the children's school and presumably were new to the children.) First, each child's reading instructional level was found. This was done by asking each child to read the words on one of the lists. If a child knew all the words on the list, he or she was given a harder list. If the child didn't know most of the words on the list, he or she was given an easier list. This continued until a list was found where the child knew most of the words but not all of the words. Next, each child was asked to read the story from which this list was derived and the words each child missed were recorded. Finally, the words each child missed on the list were compared to the words he or she missed in the story.

Amazingly, the children read words in the story that they missed on the list! That is, a child may have misread horse as "house" in the list but read it correctly in the story. On the average, the first-graders got almost two-thirds of the words they missed on the list correct in the story. The second-graders had a 75 percent gain in the story over the list. The third-graders had an 82 percent gain in the story over the list.

Could Goodman's findings have been an artifact of the research design, that the children saw the words a second time when they saw them in the story? To some extent, but not entirely. Tom Nicholson, Christine Lillas, and M. Anne Rzoska (1988) gave six- and eight-year-old good readers (children reading a year or more above their grade level) and six- and eight-year-old poor readers (children reading a year or more below their grade level) stories and words in lists, in counterbalanced order. That is, one half of the children read the story first and the list second; the other half read the list first and the story second. Nicholson and his associates found that each group of children reading at a second-grade level or below, on average read 43 percent to 52 percent of the words they missed in the list right in the stories. Only the more proficient readers, the children reading at a fourth-grade level or above, did as well on the lists as in the stories. The more proficient readers had become like us—fluent readers who can pronounce print words equally well in isolation and in context.

Goodman's findings have withstood the test of replication studies. Experimental studies have consistently found that early readers use context (Stanovich 1991, p. 431) and that they read words in the context of stories better than out of such context (Nicholson 1991).

Goodman's finding that children read print words better in the context of a story than in isolation was a breakthrough in our understanding of how children figure out new print words. If the children had used letter-sound correspondences alone to read the words, they would have read the words in the lists as well as they read them in the stories. Why did the children do so much better with the unfamiliar words when they read them in stories than when they read them in lists?

> Children read print words better in the context of a story than in isolation. In stories they have additional cues in the flow of the language.

Goodman (1965) offered an explanation that is widely accepted today. Before he did the experiment, Goodman reasoned that the children would do better in identifying unfamiliar words in the stories than in the lists because "in lists, children had only cues within printed words while in stories they had the additional cues in the flow of the language" to help them figure out new print words.

What did Goodman mean by "the flow of the language"? Let me give you an example. Pretend the sentence below has been smudged and some of the letters have been obliterated. Read the sentence and see if you can figure out the missing words anyway. (The length of the spaces is not related to the length of the words.)

The cowboy strapped the s\_\_\_\_ on the h\_\_\_\_ and r\_\_\_\_ away.

You were able to figure out the "smudged" words by using your knowledge of spoken English, your knowledge of what cowboys do, and only a few letters. It wasn't necessary to see all the letters in the words to figure out the words.

As a matter of fact, if the topic is familiar to you and the flow of the language is natural, it is possible to figure out unfamiliar print words in a print context without any letter cues. To illustrate this point, I've deleted every fifth word, beginning with the tenth word, from the passage below. See if you can figure out the words that are missing. (Again, the length of the spaces is not related to the length of the words.)

> Reading theorists rejected the traditional conception of reading as _____ process of converting print _____ spoken language and redefined _____ as a process of _____ sense of print. That _____, if a child does _____ understand what he or _____ is "reading," he or _____ is *not* reading.

Most of the blanks you filled in easily using your knowledge of spoken English. The fourth blank may, or may not, have been a little harder, depending on your familiarity with the expression "making sense of print." The point is, you were able to figure out many words—in this case, about one out of five of the words in the passage—without using any letters. You did this by using your knowledge of spoken English and your knowledge of the topic.

Suppose you had learned to recognize holistically the print words written in the above passage. Suppose also that the print words that are omitted were in fact written but unfamiliar to you. Suppose they were

> *@      *!%-      !-%      |      *%      @:;      \|>*!#

Now read the passage again and see if you can read the unfamiliar "words."

> Reading theorists rejected the traditional conception of reading as | process of converting print *!%- spoken language and redefined *% as a process of \|>*!# sense of print. That *@, if a child does !-% understand what he or @:; is "reading," he or @:; is *not* reading.

As you can see, by using your knowledge of the language and the context, you were able to figure out the unfamiliar print words without any knowledge of "letter"-sound correspondences. Now, tell me, what is the "word" !-%? Stumped? Look back to the passage and use your knowledge of English to figure it out.

In the previous paragraph, did you notice how hard it was when I asked, "What is the 'word' !-%"? Did you also notice how much easier it was when you went back to the passage and used your knowledge of English to figure out the word? (You may have also noticed that it was easier for you to read the passage on your second and third reading than on your first reading.)

## *Effective Beginning Reading Materials*

Goodman's demonstration that children use their knowledge of language to figure out print words in stories has important implications for beginning reading materials for children. Until the time of Goodman's experiment, supporters of the letter-emphasis approach advocated beginning reading materials that were based on letter-phoneme correspondences children had been taught. Likewise, supporters of the word-emphasis approach advocated beginning reading materials that were based on words children had been taught. The unfortunate consequence of both approaches was that the flow of language became unnatural and distorted. Goodman's finding suggests that children need another type of reading material—reading material in which the flow of language is natural.

This insight gave rise to a new approach to teaching children to read called the whole language approach. Of the three methods (the letter-emphasis [or phonics] approach, the word-emphasis [or whole word] approach, and the whole language approach), the whole language approach is the only one to be developed through research rather than before research.

Goodman's finding would lead us to predict that children learning to read would read text with a natural flow of language better than text with an unnatural flow of language. That is, we would guess that children learning to read would more easily read stories written in natural, whole language better than stories written in the old style, letter-emphasis and word-emphasis approaches. Lynn Rhodes (1979) tested this prediction.

Rhodes asked thirteen first-grade children to read aloud four stories. Two of the stories reflected the whole language approach, one reflected the letter-emphasis, or phonics, approach, and one reflected the word-emphasis, or whole word, approach. (Remember, in whole language the flow of the language is natural, while in the phonics and whole word approaches only letter-phoneme correspondences or words that have been taught are used.)

One of the whole language stories was *The Three Little Pigs*. While *The Three Little Pigs* had a familiar story line, the other three stories had story lines that were unfamiliar to the children before they read them. Here are samples from the four stories:

From the *whole language* text with the *familiar* story line:

Once upon a time there were three little pigs.
One day the three little pigs left home.
Each little pig wanted to build a house.
The first little pig made a house of straw.
The second little pig made a house of sticks.
The third little pig made a house of bricks.

From the *whole language* text with the *unfamiliar* story line:

He called the old woman.
The old woman pulled the old man.
The old man pulled the turnip.
They pulled—and pulled again.
But they could not pull it up.
So the old woman called her granddaughter.
The granddaughter pulled the old woman.

From the *phonics* text:

Don came to the stand.
"I want something," said Don.
"I want something to eat.
What can I get from this stand?"

From the *whole word* text:

Then Ted remembered something.
He liked applesauce with pork chops.
Sometimes Mother forgot to get the applesauce.
Ted thought, "Maybe other people forget it, too.
I can get some cans of applesauce and put them with the pork chops.
Then other mothers will not forget."

Three of the children read all four stories aloud without any difficulty. They had become like us, fluent readers who can pronounce print representing unfamiliar language as well as familiar language. Hence, only the oral readings of the ten children who experienced some difficulty in reading the materials aloud were helpful in figuring out how children learn to pronounce unfamiliar print.

Among the ten children who had some difficulty in their oral reading of the stories, Rhodes found the children read aloud the two whole language stories better than the other two stories. As you can see in Figure 3.1, while the children averaged only 10.3 and 14.3 oral reading mistakes per hundred

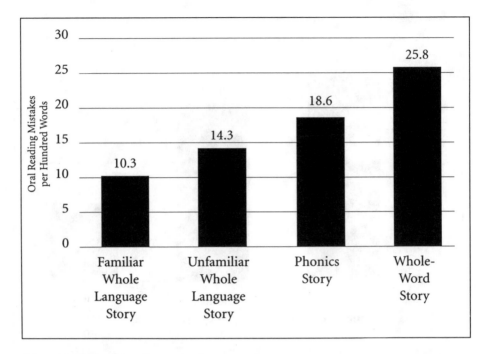

*Figure 3.1  Oral Reading Mistakes*

words on the two whole language stories, they averaged 18.6 and 25.8 mistakes per hundred words on the other two stories.

Since reading is not converting print into spoken language but making sense of print, Rhodes also asked each child to retell the stories to find out what he or she had understood. Of the three stories with the unfamiliar story line, the children did better on retelling the whole language story than the other two stories. As you can see in Figure 3.2, while the children retold an average of 60.8 percent on the whole language story, they retold an average of 51.8 percent on the phonics story and 23.9 percent on the whole word story.

You may be saying "Hey! That's not fair. The whole language story was inherently interesting and the letter-emphasis and word-emphasis stories were boring. The case was 'loaded' against the letter-emphasis and word-emphasis stories." You are right that the whole language story was more interesting than the other two stories. However, this is a consequence of the way the stories were developed. In the phonics and whole word stories the story writers were limited to letters or words that had been taught. It is much easier to create natural,

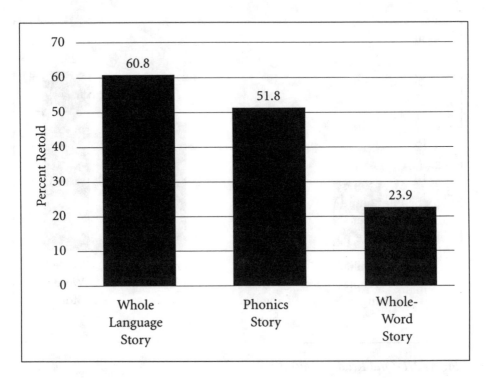

*Figure 3.2 Retelling Scores*

interesting stories when one is focusing on story plot and language than when one is limited by which letters or print words have been taught.

You might have also objected that the phonics and whole word stories were developed on the premise that children had already been taught the specific letters or words used in the two stories and the subjects of Rhodes's experiment had not. Again this is true. However, Americans are very mobile. Each year one in five American households move, and such moves almost invariably involve changing schools. Even if parents and educators could somehow guarantee that children would not move from school to school during their early years of reading instruction, who could guarantee that children would never miss school due to illness, doctors' appointments, and so forth? More important, even if the children are always present, who would guarantee that every child will learn everything he or she is taught?

Rhodes also asked the children to tell her what they liked and disliked about the stories. Their response to the whole language story with the unfamiliar story line about the turnip was particularly revealing. Although the children generally liked the whole language stories better than the other two stories, they complained about the words *turnip* and *granddaughter* in the turnip story. These were the very words in the story that violated whole language instructional principles. It is more than likely the children did not have these words in their spoken language. Turnips are not a popular vegetable with most young children. Furthermore, while children may know the word *grandmother*, they might not hear the word *granddaughter* too often.

While researchers like to involve large numbers of children in their investigations, sometimes the meaning of their findings get lost in averages. Rhodes's point that children read whole language text better than letter-emphasis, or phonics, text hit home with me in a class taught by Stephen Kucer when he shared his research (1985) findings.

First Dr. Kucer showed us the transcript of a third-grade child reading a story reflecting the phonics approach and the child's retelling of the story. Then Dr. Kucer showed us another transcript of a third-grade child reading a story reflecting the whole language approach and the child's retelling of that story. Finally Dr. Kucer asked us to judge for ourselves which set of oral readings and retellings was better.

Copies of the readings and retellings follow. (The words in brackets [ ] are words in the stories that were not read. Words between plus signs + + were added to the story during the reading.) See which set of readings and retellings you think is better.

### CHILD READING THE PHONICS STORY
### ORAL READING:

A Pin from [for] . . . a Pin for Dan. A man had a tin pin. It [it's] a . . . it's a pin of [for] a . . . pin of [for] a cup [cap]. Can Dan [Dad] wind [win] it for Dan . . . Dad wind [win] . . . win it for Dan? Dad [wins] the pin. The pin is [in] a . . . The pin is in a bag. In [on] the bag . . . on the bag is a t . . . tag. The pin first [fits] on Dan's cup [cap]. D . . . Dad pinned [pins] it on the cup [cap]. The pin is Dan's pin.

### RETELLING:

Well, his Dad was going to buy, Dan's Dad was going to buy, is going to buy a pin and his Dad bought him a pin and pinned it on his cup.

### CHILD READING THE WHOLE LANGUAGE STORY
### ORAL READING:

The Great Big Enormous Turnip. Out open on [Once upon a] time an old man planted a little t . . . turnip. The old man said "Grow, grow, li . . . little t

... turnip. Grow set [sweet]. Grow, grow little turnip. Grow st ... strong." And the turnip gro ... grew up strong [sweet] and st ... strong and big and [enormous]. Then one day the old man went to pull +to pull+ it up. He pulled—and pulled agen [again]. But he could not pull it up. He called the old woman. The o ... old woman pulled the old man. The old man pulled the turnip. And they pulled—and pulled again. But they could not pull it up. So the old woman called her granddaughter. The granddaughter pulled the old woman. The old woman pulled the old man. The old man pulled the turnip. And they pulled—and pulled again. But they could not pull it up. [The] granddaughter called the black dog. The black dog pulled the granddaughter. The granddaughter pulled the old woman. The old woman pulled the old man. The old man pulled the turnip. And they pulled—and pulled again. But they could not pull it up. The black dog called the cat. The cat pulls [pulled] +on+ the dog. The dog pulls [pulled] +on+ the granddaughter. The granddaughter pulls [pulled] +on+ the old woman. The old woman pulls [pulled] on the [old] man. The [old] man pulls [pulled] +on+ the turnip. And they pulled—and pulled again. But they still could not pull it up. The cat called the mouse +and+ the mouse pulled +on+ the cat. The cat pulled +on+ the dog. The dog pulled +on+ the granddaughter. The grand-daughter pulled +on+ the old woman. The old woman pulled +on+ the [old] man. The [old] man pulled the turnip. a ... They pulled—and pulled again. And up came the turnip at last!

### RETELLING:

On an open prairie there was a man and he started digging and he dug on the turnip and he pulled on the turnip and he couldn't and he called the old woman. The old woman pulled on him, but they couldn't do it and then the old woman called the granddaughter and the granddaughter pulled the old woman and the man and they still could not do it, pull the turnip up and then the granddaughter called the black dog. The black dog, the granddaughter, the old woman and the old man pulled on it, but they still could not get it so the black dog went and got a cat and the cat pulled on the black dog and the black dog pulled on the granddaughter and the granddaughter pulled on the old woman, the old woman pulled on the man and the man pulled on the turnip. But they still could not get it out. The cat ran out and got a mouse and then the mouse pulled on the cat, the cat pulled on the dog, the dog pulled on the granddaughter, the grand-daughter pulled on the old woman, the old woman pulled on the old man, the old man pulled on the turnip and then, a little after they pulled it popped out and they all fell down.

Which reading-and-retelling do you think was better? We students concluded that the reading-and-retelling by the child reading the whole language story about the turnip was better than that of the child reading the phonics story about the pin, once the child reading the whole language story got beyond the beginning of the story. Notice, for example, how in line six of the turnip story the child had trouble with the word *again*, but as she got into the story and encountered *again* four times later she did fine.

In one type of reading material the child did poorly. In the other, the same child did well.

After we reached our conclusion, Dr. Kucer told us that it was the same child who had done both readings and retellings. What a difference a child's reading materials make! In one type of reading material the child did poorly. In the other, the same child did well.

The letter- and word-emphasis stories that the children in Rhodes' and Kucer's studies struggled with belong to a type of reading materials for early readers called *decodable stories*. Decodable stories are limited to the words or word parts that children have been taught, so children can then practice what they have been taught.

The whole language story *The Great Big Enormous Turnip*, which the children in Rhodes's and Kucer's studies read so successfully, belongs to another type of reading materials for early readers called *predictable stories* (Rhodes 1981). Some, like *The Great Big Enormous Turnip*, have repetitive refrains. Most are bound as individual books. However, what really distinguishes predictable stories from their predecessors is that (1) the language of the stories is familiar to children, and (2) the pictures and print are redundant; that is, the print tells a whole, coherent story independent of the pictures, and the pictures, to the extent possible, represent the story told by the print. These two elements, in combination with a teaching technique called *shared reading* (described in the next section), enable children to use what they know—spoken language—to learn about what they don't know—written language.

# Effective Beginning Reading Instruction

Goodman's demonstration that children use their knowledge of language to figure out print words in stories has important implications for reading instruction as well as for reading materials. Goodman's findings would lead us to predict that children would learn to read better when teaching focuses on overall story meaning rather than on words or word parts. Teaching that focuses on overall story meaning invites children to use their knowledge of language and the world to figure out print.

Richard Anderson, Ian Wilkinson, and Jana Mason (1991) conducted an experiment that compared the effectiveness of teaching that focuses on meaning with teaching that does not focus on meaning. They asked six third-grade teachers to teach two lessons with an emphasis on overall story meaning and two lessons with an emphasis on such things as word analysis and accurate oral reading. They found that the lessons that emphasized overall story meaning led to better outcomes in relation to factors such as students' recall, oral reading, story interest, and lesson time. While all of the reading groups—high, average, and low—benefited from the emphasis on meaning, the average and low groups especially benefited from it.

The National Assessment of Educational Progress (NAEP) asked fourth-grade teachers across the U.S. to characterize their reading instruction and then compared the teachers' responses with the students' scores on standardized tests in reading (Mullis, Campbell, and Farstrup 1993, p. 30). As can be seen in Figure 3.3, students whose reading instruction emphasized *whole language* clearly outscored students whose reading instruction emphasized *phonics*; students whose reading instruction had little or no emphasis on phonics outscored students whose reading instruction emphasized phonics.

You might say, "Perhaps an emphasis on meaning is helpful to third-

| Instruction | Heavy Emphasis | Moderate Emphasis | Little/No Emphasis |
|---|---|---|---|
| Whole Language | 220 | 218 | 218 |
| Phonics | 208 | 218 | 222 |

*Figure 3.3 Average Reading Proficiency Scores of Students, Grade 4, by Instructional Emphasis*

and fourth-grade children who have already had several years of reading instruction. How about children who have not had a lot of reading instruction? How about kindergartners or first-grade children?"

Helene Ribowsky (1986) studied two kindergarten classes where one class had a whole language reading program and one had a letter-emphasis, or phonics, reading program. She found that the children in the whole language program became better early readers at the end of the school year than the children in the phonics program. Not only that, the children in the class with the whole language program also developed a better awareness of phonemes than the children in the class with the phonics program.

Ray Reutzel and Robert Cooter (1990) did a similar study with first-graders. They compared two first-grade classes that had a whole language reading program with two first-grade classes that had a traditional reading program built on whole word and phonics instructional practices. They found that the children in the two whole language classes became significantly better readers at the end of the school year than the children in the traditional classes.

Penny Freepon (1991) also compared children in two first-grade classes with a whole language reading program with children in two first-grade classes with traditional whole word and phonics reading programs. She had similar findings. In Freepon's study the children in the two whole language classrooms not only had a better sense that reading was constructing meaning with print but also were almost twice as successful as the children in the traditional classrooms at sounding out words.

"Okay," you say. "Perhaps an emphasis on meanings is helpful for mainstream children. How about disadvantaged and at-risk children? Don't they need phonics instruction?" As we will see in Chapter 7, Dina Feitelson, Bracha Kita, and Zahava Goldstein (1986) studied a first-grade class of disadvantaged children who were read to from series stories for the last twenty minutes of the school day for six months. The children in the class became more interested in reading for pleasure and acquired more personal books. Half the children in the class spontaneously bought or borrowed copies of the series books and read them during their breaks and free time at school. Feitelson and her colleagues found that at the end of the six-month study, the children in the class that had been read to outscored children in the control classes that had not been read to in both their ability to pronounce print and in their reading comprehension.

"Okay," you say. "But how about poor readers? Don't they need phonics instruction so they can learn to read?" Recall that the average and low readers in Anderson's experiment benefited from the meaning-emphasis lessons more than the lessons that emphasized word analysis. Margaret Richek and

Becky McTague (1988) had similar findings with second- and third-grade struggling readers. McTague taught children in a remedial reading program to read whole print words in the context of the continuous text of popular children's books thirty minutes a day for eighteen school days. At the end of eighteen days (or nine hours) of instruction, without instruction in phonics, the children who had learned to read whole print words in context did much better in oral reading and comprehension of new reading materials than the control group—another group of children of identical age and reading level who had continued the district's whole word plus phonics program during the same period of time.

"Okay," you say. "But how about nonnative speakers of English, children learning English as a subsequent language? Wouldn't phonics instruction help them?" Warwick Elley (1991) reviewed nine studies of elementary school children learning English as a subsequent language. Groups engaged in meaning-based encounters with literacy were compared with control groups receiving traditional instruction. Again the students in the meaning-based programs did better on standardized measures of reading, including word identification and phonics skills.

Studies like these by Rhodes, Kucer, Anderson and his associates, the NAEP, Ribowsky, Reutzel and Cooter, Freepon, Feitelson and her colleagues, Richek and McTague, Elley, and many others have convinced many researchers and teachers that a meaning-emphasis, whole language approach to reading instruction is more helpful to children than our traditional methods.

How, you might ask, do teachers teach early readers to read print in the context of continuous text? Let me give you some examples.

One way is the *Language Experience Approach* (Lee and Van Allen 1963). In this technique, which is quite old, teachers and children share a common experience such as doing a science experiment or seeing a movie on a social studies topic. The teacher then invites the children to talk about the common experience and writes down the children's words as they tell about the experience. Then the teacher teaches the children to read what they have said by reading the text *to* the children while pointing to the words in full view of the children. Next, the teacher reads the text *with* the children. Finally the teacher invites the children to read the passage *by themselves*.

Another technique is *shared reading*, originally developed by Don Holdaway (1979). In shared reading the teacher uses a predictable story in a big book—an oversize book with oversize print. (As we saw in the previous section, a predictable story is a whole, coherent story written in language familiar to children where the pictures, as much as possible, represent the story told by the print.) First the teacher introduces the book to the children by reading the title and the names of the author and illustrator while pointing to the print and then discussing the pictures in the story with the children. Then the teacher reads the story *to* the children while pointing to the words in full view of the children. After several readings (possibly over several consecutive days), the teacher reads the story *with* the children. Then, when the children have memorized the language of the text, the teacher invites the children to "read" the story *by themselves*, both as a whole group looking at the big book and then with reading partners working with "little books," smaller versions of the big book. The children's memory of the language of the story and the pictures in the text guide the children's reading of the text.

Still another way to help early readers read stories is *assisted reading*. Margaret Richek and Becky McTague (1988) used assisted reading with struggling second- and third-grade readers. On the first day of the study, McTague read several pages of a popular children's story *to* the children. Then she read the story again *with* the children but stopped at highly predictable words and let the children take over. Next she let the children read the story *by themselves*. Finally the children dictated their own version of the story to McTague and she wrote the children's version of the story and helped the children read it. The following day the activities were repeated with the next several pages in the book. The succeeding days were similar, with McTague gradually providing less and less support as the children indicated they didn't need it any more. As McTague and the children finished one book they went on to other books in the series.

Yet another method of helping early readers read in the context of continuous print is to provide them with *CD-ROM interactive stories*. CD-ROM interactive stories such as those developed by *Discus* and the *Learning Company's Reading Development Library* series are very helpful for intermediate (fourth and fifth) grade struggling readers. When only one child is at the computer at a time, the child can click on any word he or she does not recognize while reading and the computer will pronounce the unfamiliar word for the child.

In my research I observed a fourth-grade child change from a struggling reader to an empowered reader when she worked in three forty-five minute sessions at a computer with a CD-ROM. Before the child worked on the computer she was able to read, in a faltering voice, about 80 percent of the words in a first-grade story. The first session at the computer I showed her how to click on words to get help. Initially she used the computer to assist her reading. By the third session at the computer she also used the computer to confirm her reading. She would click on a word she had read correctly, hear the computer confirm her reading, and joyously say, "I knew that!" If she lost the meaning, she would say "That don't make no sense" and return to the point where she thought the confusion began and click on the word. She also read fluently with natural intonation rather than the "flat" intonation she had had without the computer. She showed she was comprehending the text by commenting on the story line as she read, with remarks such as "Goldilocks shouldn't have done that!" Subsequent research with other children suggested that at least some of the factors that made this experience successful for this child were that (1) she had acquired an intrinsic motivation to learn to read through being read to in school and (2) her efforts to teach herself to read at the computer were supported by a teacher knowledgeable in recent research findings about how children learn to read.

Would a struggling reader be transformed to a grade-level reader after a few sessions, or even a few weeks, at the computer? No, but he or she would be given a powerful lift on the road to becoming a grade-level reader. Presumably more time at the computer, combined with opportunities to read interesting, age-appropriate stories with familiar language would lead to even more competency off the computer.

Which of these techniques is more effective? They are all necessary tools for teachers. The Language Experience Approach helps children understand that what can be said can be written and what can be written can be read. Shared reading with predictable books demonstrates the reading process to early readers and helps early readers become more proficient readers. Teachers can use assisted reading with early readers who have had multiple experiences with predictable stories as a bridge to help them move on to reading less predictable stories. Finally teachers can use assisted reading and CD-ROM interactive stories to help struggling readers who have not had the advantage of extensive shared reading with predictable stories in kindergarten and first grades.

While teachers need to have all of these tools at their disposal, over time the single most important of these instructional strategies for the purpose of teaching reading, in my experience and the experience of knowledgeable colleagues, is shared reading with predictable stories. Shared reading of lots of predictable stories with knowledgeable teachers is a powerful and effective way to launch children into lifelong reading. Extensive, pleasant experiences with shared reading with predictable stories enables children to see themselves as readers and to become readers more quickly and more easily than any other single experience teachers can provide.

The work of Goodman, Rhodes, Kucer, and others has helped us understand how children use their knowledge of language to figure out unfamiliar print words. However, something was missing in the explanation. If readers *use* letter-sound correspondences to read, how do they *learn* letter-sound correspondences? This is a question whole language theory has not been able to answer until now. Now it can be answered. That is the topic of Chapter 5.

However, before we answer the question of how children learn letter-sound correspondences, we need to shift our focus from children's thinking back to adults' thinking and see the consequences of not having been able to answer this question until now. We need to look at the groan zone.

# 4

# The Groan Zone

## *Maintaining Tradition*

Research findings such as those outlined in Chapter 2 as well as classroom experience informed many researchers and some practitioners that children have trouble analyzing spoken words into phonemes. These same researchers and practitioners were excited about the research findings on the invisible—or linguistic and cognitive—systems in reading and learning to read summarized in Chapter 3. Once again letter-phoneme instruction was de-emphasized, in theory if not in practice.

Although these researchers and practitioners were uncomfortable, for good reason, with the traditional explanation of how children learn a letter-sound system, they did not have an alternative explanation of how children learn the visible (or letter-sound) system other than via traditional phonics instruction. While acknowledging that readers use their knowledge of both the visible and the invisible systems in learning to read, they emphasized the invisible systems. This emphasis on the invisible systems made those who believe that children learn to read by learning the sounds of letters uncomfortable.

A case in point is California, the state where I live and teach. While California is but one state in the nation, its story has national significance. As the most populous state, and one with statewide textbook adoption policies, California has the largest textbook market in the nation. What California approves for its schools to buy with state money affects what publishers publish and hence what is available for schools in other states to buy.

In California every seven years knowledgeable educators in each curricular area revise the state curriculum framework in their area of expertise. The year following the framework adoption year is the textbook adoption year. During the textbook adoption year publishers submit instructional materials for evaluation; another group of educators with expertise in the curriculum area evaluate the materials according to criteria set forth in the framework and submit recommendations to the state board of education. The board then adopts a list of approved materials (California Department of Education 1988). Until recently, at least 80 percent of the materials that school districts purchased with state money had to be selected from the approved materials list unless districts applied for a waiver.[1]

In 1986, educators across the state, chosen for their expertise in reading and writing education, wrote an English-language arts curriculum framework for California's public schools, kindergarten through twelfth grade, consistent with the best of what we then knew about how children learn to read. The curriculum principles they outlined for elementary schools emphasized the invisible systems in learning to read and called for the visible system, phonics, to be "taught in meaningful contexts, kept simple, and completed in the early grades" (California Department of Education 1987, p. 4). The effect of this framework was to discourage the purchase of phonics workbooks where letter-sound correspondences are taught with little or no meaningful context.

The trouble was most teachers and parents either did not know about, or did not understand, the research findings on the invisible systems children use in learning to read. Presumably the state superintendent of public instruction at that time did not either, for there was minimal support to help teachers and parents understand the new, counterintuitive concepts underlying the framework. Teachers and parents who equated phonics instruction with learning to read were perplexed by the new reading curriculum. Once again the public was concerned about de-emphasizing phonics instruction. This time the United States government got involved.

Responding to the concerns of its constituents in California and

---

[1]Until recently, districts who applied for a waiver to use state money to buy materials not on the adoption list were routinely granted permission to do so. Now, according to Veltema (1997, p. 18), "Although the waiver system to purchase other materials is still built into the legislation, it has essentially been rendered null and void except for the purchase of library books." Additionally, the California Board of Education decided to audit school districts' training funds and force districts to return state money if they do not follow the state's new direction on phonics (Weintraub 1997, pp. 1, 6).

elsewhere, Congress asked the U.S. Department of Education to issue a request for research on phonics. The request was not to ask whether traditional phonics should be taught to beginning readers but how it should be taught systematically (Adams 1990, pp. 28–29). Marilyn Adams of Bolt Beranek and Newman, Inc., a private profit-making research group in Cambridge, Massachusetts, was commissioned to do the job. Adams's "findings," embodied in *Beginning to Read*, were determined before she was commissioned to write the book.

In *Beginning to Read* Adams reported the findings by Bruce, by Rosner, by Liberman and her colleagues, by Ehri and Wilce, by Mann, by Treiman and Baron, by Tunmer and Nesdale, and by others that children have trouble analyzing spoken words into phonemes. In fact, all the research I report in Chapter 2 is reported in Adams's book. Adams also reported Treiman's findings that even adults have difficulty analyzing spoken words into phonemes (Adams 1990, p. 314; Treiman 1983, 1985, 1986). Yet, rather than questioning whether children need to analyze spoken words into phonemes in order to read, Adams maintained, as she was commissioned to do, that we must teach children to analyze spoken words into phonemes so that they can read. (An interesting case of making the child fit the theory despite the facts.) The book popularized the term phonemic awareness, or PA, a term used to describe a person's ability to analyze spoken words into phonemes. The conclusion of the book—that children need to have phonemic awareness to learn to read—is compatible with our two-millennium-old assumption that children learn to read by learning letters. It is not compatible with research findings that children have difficulty in analyzing spoken words into phonemes.

Back in California, as the seven-year cycle on the *English-Language Arts Framework* was coming to an end, the Curriculum Commission reviewed the framework. The Commission "affirmed that the 1986 framework[2] still contains valid and current instructional principles and should not be revised [during the 1994–1995 framework adoption year]. However, the Curriculum Commission recognized that teachers need more time to implement the many changes in the 1986 framework" (California Department of Education 1987/1994, p. viii).

Then suddenly, in 1995 the news media was abuzz with stories that

---

[2]The framework was approved by the Curriculum Commission in 1986 but published in 1987. Hence, some documents refer to it as the 1986 framework and others refer to it as the 1987 framework.

California's children were not reading at "basic" levels. The evidence was the NAEP report prepared by the Educational Testing Service under contract with the U.S. Department of Education. In 1992 the Educational Testing Service administered a standardized test in reading to representative schools in participating states at grades four, eight, and twelve. It then issued a "national reading report card." Since only the fourth-grade scores were reported by state, state-by-state comparisons could be made only at the fourth-grade level. While California's fourth-grade children clearly were not failing to learn to read, California did have a greater proportion of children who were less proficient English readers than forty of the forty-two other participating states and territories. In fact, the average reading proficiency for California's fourth-graders was in the bottom 20 percent of the nation in every demographic category (race, gender, size and type of community, and parental educational level) except advantaged urban (Mullis, Campbell, and Farstrup 1993, p. 29). What could have been the cause?

The facts that California had the largest (or next to largest, depending on which year one counts) class size in the nation and that class size affects academic outcomes (Wood et al. 1990; Nye et al. 1992) were ignored. The facts that California's elementary school libraries are among the poorest in the nation (White 1990) and access to age-appropriate books affects academic outcomes (Elley 1994; Krashen 1995) were ignored. The facts that California's non-Hispanic white and African American children's reading scores matched those of other states in the western region[3] but that California's Hispanic children, the fastest-growing group in California, had the lowest average of any ethnic group in any state, including the other border states (Mullis et al. 1993, p. 25) were ignored. The facts that 25 percent of California's population consists of new immigrants (Associated Press 1995; Knight 1997) and that most of these new immigrants are Spanish-speaking were ignored. The facts that the NAEP test does not distinguish between native speakers of English and children who are learning English as a subsequent language, and that it usually takes children learning English as a subsequent-language who have the advantage of instruction in their home language five to seven years to achieve in English at levels

---

[3]The western states in the NAEP report are states west of and including Montana, Wyoming, Colorado, Oklahoma, and Texas. California's advantaged urban and disadvantaged urban students, as a whole, were achieving at higher levels than other states in the Western Region (Mullis et al. 1993, 27).

comparable to native English-speaking children[4] were ignored. Finally, the facts that only 2 percent of the state's teachers had been exposed to whole language principles and the California Department of Education was still compiling a book of sample lesson plans (Colvin 1995a) were ignored.

Whole language and the *English-Language Arts Framework* that "teachers needed more time to implement" were blamed. The "failure" of whole language in California was cited as justification for changes in other states (Chen and Colvin 1996).

One way to identify strengths and weaknesses in our educational system is to compare children's reading achievements state by state. Another way is to compare children's reading achievements country by country. The IEA (International Association for the Evaluation of Educational Achievement) compared children's reading achievement in thirty-two countries (Elley 1992; Binkley and Williams 1996). The IEA study found that fourth-graders in the U.S. tied with Sweden in second place behind fourth-graders in Finland. By ninth grade the children of France, New Zealand, Hungary, Iceland, Switzerland, Hong Kong, Singapore, Slovenia, Germany, Portugal, and Canada tied with the United States for second place behind Finland.

Given these findings we have to wonder if we have a crisis in literacy education in the United States as some suggest . . . or if we have a manufactured crisis as David Berliner and Bruce Biddle (1995) suggest. We also have to wonder, given that the children of fourteen other countries catch up with the children of the United States and Sweden by ninth grade, if there is any lasting value in being ahead in fourth grade. Also, we have to wonder what we might discover if we knew how California's children learning English as a subsequent language were doing by ninth grade? Finally, we might question why a score of 212, not 200 or some other number, on the NAEP test was chosen as the score children have to reach to be classified as reading at a "basic" level.

Another way to identify the strengths and weaknesses of our educational system is to compare how well we did in the past with how well we are doing now. The Rand Corporation compared students' achievement in 1970 and 1995 (Hanania 1995). They found reading and math achievement are higher today than in 1970 among all groups, with African American and Hispanic children making the greatest gains. They concluded that we should be skeptical about scare headlines in the media because, although we need to

---

[4]Collier (1989). The NAEP scores do not include children learning English as a subsequent language their first two years in the U.S. (Mullis et al. 1993, p. xx). However, as Collier's data show, children learning English as a subsequent language need more than two years to catch up with their native English-speaking peers academically.

continue improving our schools, the average student in the United States to-day can read, write, and solve mathematical problems better than ever.

Nevertheless, California's new superintendent of public instruction, elected in 1994, called for "balanced reading instruction" to correct the "literacy crisis." She said children need both good literature and instruction in phonics. She convened (or more precisely, had a concerned but unqualified citizen who is an active proponent of traditional phonics instruction convene [Colvin 1995b]) a Reading Task Force to make recommendations for California's reading program.

The committee that wrote the 1987 *English-Language Arts Framework* was composed of experienced educators with expertise in reading and writing education. In contrast, approximately half of the Reading Task Force consisted of concerned citizens whose experience and expertise in teaching reading and writing in kindergarten through third-grade classrooms was not apparent, for example, a vice president of TRW, Inc., a vice president of Sony Pictures Entertainment, an analyst of RPP International, Inc., a liaison to the governor's office, two school board members,[5] a community member (the convener of the committee), two foundation heads, and two parents. While the educators on the task force were impressive (e.g., three superintendents, three professors of literacy education), their involvement in teaching reading and writing in kindergarten through third-grade classrooms was also not apparent. Of the three elementary school educators on the task force at the time it met, one was a principal, one was a fourth-grade teacher, and one was a special-education teacher. Not one member of the task force was a kindergarten, first-, second-, or third-grade classroom teacher.

The research that showed the mind-boggling complexity of our letter-sound system was ignored. The research showing that children have difficulty analyzing spoken words into phonemes was forgotten. In its report, *Every Child a Reader,* the Reading Task Force "concluded that the 1987 *English-Language Arts Framework* did not present a comprehensive and balanced reading program and gave insufficient attention to a systematic skills instructional program" (California Department of Education 1995, p. 2). The task force recommended, among other things, "an organized, explicit skills program that includes phonemic awareness (sounds in words), phonics, and decoding skills to address the needs of the emergent reader" (p. 2). The task force also recommended, "Every elementary classroom should have at least 1,500 books so that there is a sufficient supply of age-appropriate books and

---

[5]School board members typically do not have professional preparation in education.

stories in all grades" (p. 10). As we will see, the first recommendation has been taken quite seriously. The second recommendation has yet to be implemented or viewed as the responsibility of the educational system.

The English-language arts textbook adoption process continued on cycle. During the textbook adoption year of 1995–1996, 110 educators were selected for their knowledge in reading and writing instruction. Using the criteria established by the framework the California State Board of Education had renewed for a second seven-year cycle during the 1994–1995 adoption year, these educators reviewed language arts programs that had been submitted for adoption. They then recommended to the state board programs that, in their professional judgment, met the criteria.

Then, in a highly unusual move, the state board of education removed two programs from the list. These programs were the publishing industry's pacesetters in predictable stories for shared reading.

The state board made another unusual move. Two years into the second seven-year cycle of the 1987 *English-Language Arts Framework* and a year after it had convened the textbook adoption committee, the state board convened another group of teachers to write a new English-language arts framework.

Meanwhile, as the 1995 Reading Task Force was meeting, Assembly Bill 170 passed through the California Assembly and Senate unopposed. AB 170 requires that elementary school reading textbooks include phonics and spelling. The following year other laws were passed, among them AB 1178 and AB 3482. AB 1178 requires that before teacher candidates receive their preliminary teaching credential they must pass a test in reading instruction that includes direct, systematic, explicit phonics. AB 3482 "appropriates $152 million (approximately $80 per pupil in kindergarten through third grade) to ensure that every child in the primary grades has a full set of core reading program instructional materials. . . . The materials must (a) include systematic, explicit phonics and spelling, (b) include emphasis on phonemic awareness and (c) include reading materials that provide practice in the skill being taught" (California State Board of Education 1996, p. 6).

The governor committed $200 million from the federal Goals 2000 program to improving reading instruction. To date this money has been used to provide in-service instruction for teachers and their supervising administrators on—you guessed it—explicit, systematic, extensive (traditional) phonics (Bay 1996).

Between the spring of 1995 and the fall of 1996 the state of California moved from a call for "balanced" reading instruction to a position of actively discouraging, via AB 3482, reading materials that enable children to use their knowledge of language to figure out print. Needless to say, the sales of phonics workbooks are up in California.

Similar efforts to institutionalize, or reinstitutionalize, traditional phonics instruction are occurring in other states (Bay 1996) as well as in England, Australia, and New Zealand.

## The Underlying Problem

In spite of the findings that teaching children letter-phoneme correspondences was fraught with problems—ranging from the complexity of the task to children's inability to distinguish phonemes the same way literate adults do—some researchers and educational leaders continue to advocate that children be taught letter-phoneme correspondences. Why?

One reason is that researchers such as Jeanne Chall (1967), Guy Bond and Robert Dykstra (1967), Isabelle Liberman and her colleagues (1974), and many others kept finding that children who do well on tests that assess their knowledge of letters, phonemes, and letter-phoneme correspondences tend to be more proficient readers. (See Adams [1990] for a review of others.) Conversely, children who do less well on these same tests tend to be less proficient readers. Perhaps because we have traditionally assumed that children learn to read by being taught sounds associated with single letters and digraphs, we have interpreted these findings to mean that letter-phoneme knowledge enables children to pronounce written words.

The problem with this interpretation is that correlation does not establish causation. When two events co-occur, or occur together, one does not necessarily cause the other. People who teach statistics and research methods typically have a story to illustrate this point. One of my favorite stories is by William Michaels, formerly of the University of Southern California. Dr. Michaels tells of a time in his life when his car radio worked just fine except when he gave a ride to a coworker. After Dr. Michaels has his audience half believing the coworker's presence caused his radio to malfunction, he adds that he gave the coworker a ride only on rainy days. On those days the rain leaked into his car and his radio didn't work. Hence, the cause of the radio malfunctioning was not the coworker but the rain.

In short, we cannot infer causation from correlational research. We cannot infer from research that shows a correlation between children's letter-phoneme knowledge and their reading ability that children need to learn the sounds of letters in order to read. But researchers know that correlation does not establish causation. Hence, correlational research findings are probably not the basic reason researchers have continued to advocate instruction in letter-phoneme correspondences.

Another possible reason that some researchers and educational leaders continue to advocate that children be taught letter-phoneme correspondences despite the research findings may be a matter of tradition. As children most of us were taught letter-phoneme correspondences and urged to "sound out" words. Perhaps we grew to believe that "sounding out" words helps us figure out unfamiliar words. In my research, which I describe in the next chapter, I found that many first-grade children silently moved their lips when they encountered the unusual print words I asked them to pronounce (Moustafa 1990). They appeared to believe they were "sounding out" words when, in fact, my data shows they were not using letter-phoneme correspondences to pronounce unfamiliar words. However, traditions change, and each of us has outgrown many of the things that as children we assumed were true. Hence, instructional tradition is probably not what prompts some researchers and educational leaders to advocate instruction in letter-phoneme correspondences either.

The reason why some researchers and educational leaders continue to advocate that we teach children letter-phoneme correspondences, despite the problems we discussed above, is suggested by Thomas Kuhn (1970) in his book, *The Structure of Scientific Revolutions*. Kuhn surveyed the history of the physical sciences from ancient Greece to the present. He found that no scientific theory, no matter how badly discredited, was ever abandoned until a new theory was in place. Applying this principle to reading instruction, we can infer that some researchers and educational leaders continue to advocate that children be taught letter-phoneme correspondences because we have no other viable theory of how children acquire an alphabetic system.

Now we have a new theory of how children acquire an alphabetic system. This theory explains how the children who were learning to read stories with familiar language in the studies by the NAEP, Ribowsky, Reutzel and Cooter, Freepon, Feitelson and her colleagues, Richek and McTague, and Elley were better able to pronounce unfamiliar print than those who received more instruction in traditional phonics. I will explain this new theory in the next chapter.

# 5

# How Children Use Their Knowledge of Spoken Sounds to Pronounce Unfamiliar Print

## *Children's Perception of Sounds in Spoken Words Revisited*

In Chapter 2 we discussed evidence that young children have difficulty analyzing spoken words into phonemes. (Remember phonemes are units of sound in spoken words that are represented by single letters such as *c, k, u,* or *e*, or pairs of letters, called digraphs, such as *ck* or *ue.*) What appears obvious to us, as literate adults, is not at all obvious to young children. How, we asked, can children understand instruction in letter-phoneme correspondences if they have difficulty analyzing spoken words into phonemes?

That was the bad news. Now here is the good news. There is another way for children to learn letter-sound correspondences. Recently linguists and psychologists have discovered other units of speech intermediate between phonemes and syllables. They call these units the psychological units of syllables. What are these units? Let me explain.

Have you noticed when people make a slip of the tongue they come out with crazy things such as *With this wing I thee red* for *With this ring I thee wed*? Such slips of the tongue are called spoonerisms after William Spooner, an English cleric known for making such misstatements.

In 1972 Donald MacKay pointed out that when people make these slips of the tongue the point of division in the syllables they mix tends to be before the vowels. This led him to suggest that spoken syllables consist of two natural parts: (1) any consonants that *may* come before the vowel and (2) an

41

obligatory vowel and any consonants which *may* come after it. For example, the natural units of *wed* are /w/ and /ed/.

These natural parts of the English syllable have become known as *onsets* and *rimes*. The first part is called the onset and the last part is called the rime. Hence, in *wed* the /w/ is the onset and the /ed/ is the rime. While all spoken English syllables have a rime, not all spoken English syllables have an onset.[1]

Figure 5.1 shows examples of onsets and rimes in some one-syllable words. Notice, in the first two words in the figure, *I* and *tie*, there is only one phoneme in each onset and rime. In words such as these, onsets and rimes consist of single phonemes and it is immaterial whether we call them phonemes or onsets and rimes. However, in the last four words in the figure, *I'm*, *time*, *try*, and *crimes*, there is more than one phoneme in either the onset or the rime or both. It is in words such as these that the discovery of onsets and rimes helps us understand English-speaking children's perceptions of sounds in spoken words.

But I'm getting ahead of myself. First, we need to ask, "Can children analyze spoken words into onsets and rimes?" Rebecca Treiman (1983, 1985) was the first to ask this question. Treiman played word games with eight-year-old children and with adults. She found the children were able to split syllables into onsets and rimes. She also found that "even with training, eight-year-olds as well as adults have difficulty splitting [spoken] syllables anywhere but between their onsets and rimes." Treiman suggests that children first learn to analyze spoken syllables into onsets and rimes and later learn to analyze onsets and rimes into their constituent phonemes.

While there is a large body of research that shows children have trouble analyzing spoken words into phonemes before they begin to read, there is a growing body of research that shows young children analyze spoken words into onsets and rimes even *before* they begin to read (Goswami and Bryant 1990).[2] One of my favorites is a study done by Robert Calfee (1977).[3] Calfee told five- and six-year-old children: "When I say *greet*, you say *eat*; when I say *ties*, you say *eyes*." Although Calfee was not studying onsets and rimes, he was, in effect, asking the children to delete the onsets. The children did very well on

---

[1]While onset-rime theory applies to English, it does not apply to all languages. For example, Arabic syllables consist of an obligatory consonant-vowel sequence plus up to two optional consonants; Spanish syllables may begin with a consonant or a vowel, but when they begin with a consonant, the initial consonant and vowel cannot be divided.

[2]See Chapters 1–4 for an excellent review and analysis of the literature.

[3]Thanks to Goswami and Bryant (1990) for this reanalysis of Calfee's work.

| | Spoken Word | |
| Written Word | Onset | Rime |
| --- | --- | --- |
| I | | /i/ |
| tie | /t/ | /i/ |
| I'm | | /im/ |
| time | /t/ | /im/ |
| try | /tr/ | /i/ |
| crimes | /cr/ | /imz/ |

*Figure 5.1  Examples of Onsets and Rimes*

this task. In fact, they were right in over 90 percent of the practice tries. That is, they were able to manipulate onsets and rimes without being taught to do so.

When you think about it, it isn't all that surprising that children can manipulate onsets and rimes. Perhaps you remember speaking pig latin with your friends when you were a child. If you did, you were manipulating onsets and rimes. You took the onset of a word and put it after the rest of the word and added an /a/ sound. When the first syllable didn't have an onset, you just added /a/ to the end of the word. If you wanted to tell your friends in pig latin that reading is making sense of print, you said "eading-ray is-ay aking-may ense-say of-ay int-pray." In order to move the initial onset to the end of the word you had to first be able to analyze the first syllable into its onset and rime.

> Children manipulate onsets and rimes without being taught to do so.

I bet those of you who spoke pig latin when you were children did not learn it from your teachers but from your friends. I also bet your friends didn't give you an abstract explanation such as "you take the onset of a word, put it at the end of the word, and add an /a/ sound." They just gave you examples and you figured out how to do it from the examples. No wonder linguists call onsets and rimes the psychological units of syllables.

## Another Way of Making Letter-Sound Correspondences

The discovery of onsets and rimes raises the possibility that children do not have to analyze spoken words in phonemes to learn letter-sound correspondences. They can use onsets and rimes instead.

One indication that children use onsets and rimes rather than phonemes to learn letter-sound correspondences is Richard Wylie and Donald Durrell's (1970) study of first-grade children's ability to pronounce letters representing rimes (such as *-ock* in *rock*, *lock*, *dock*, and *clock*) as opposed to their ability to pronounce letters representing phonemes within rimes (such as *o* in *ock*).[4] Wylie and Durrell showed the children sets of letters that represent rimes such as *-ack*, *-eck*, *-ick*, *-ock*, and *-uck* and asked the children to do things like "Circle the one that says /ok/" and "Circle the one that has an /o/ in it." (In the first example they said the sound represented by *-ock* in *rock*. In the second example they said the sound represented by *o* in *rock*.)

> Children use their ability to hear onsets and rimes to make letter-sound correspondences.

Wylie and Durrell found the children were much more successful in identifying letters representing rimes than in identifying letters representing phonemes in rimes. That is, they were better at identifying the sounds of letters representing whole rimes such as /ok/ than at identifying the sounds of letters representing phonemes within rimes such as /o/ in *-ock*.

While Treiman's and Calfee's work suggests that children have a natural

---

[4]At the time Wylie and Durrell did their study, onsets and rimes had not yet been described, much less named. Wylie and Durrell called the letter strings they studied "phonograms." Phonograms are also called "word families." For simplicity, I refer to phonograms as "letters that represent rimes."

ability to hear onsets and rimes, Wylie and Durrell's work suggests that children use their ability to hear onsets and rimes to make letter-sound correspondences. Having found this, we are now ready to unlock the secret of how children use letter-sound correspondences to pronounce unfamiliar print words.

## Still Another Way of Figuring Out Unfamiliar Print Words

In 1986, two decades after Goodman demonstrated that children use their knowledge of language to figure out unfamiliar print words, Usha Goswami demonstrated, in another ingenious experiment, that kindergarten-age, first-grade-age, and second-grade-age children use their knowledge of how to say some print words to figure out how to say other print words. Before she met with the children Goswami made a list of pairs of print words. Some of the pairs—such as *hark-lark* and *hark-harm*—had common letters in the same sequences; others had common letters in different sequences.

Then Goswami met with each child, one by one. First she gave each child a pretest to find out which of her print words each child already knew how to pronounce. Then she showed each child the print words in pairs. She told each child one of the words in the pair and then asked the child to tell her the other word in the pair. She didn't tell the children how to figure out the other word in the pair.

When Goswami told the children one of the print words in the pairs, the children who didn't know the other word in the pretest but had begun to read were often able to figure out how to say the other word in the pair when the words had common letter sequences. That is, the children were able to make analogies between known and unknown print words when the words shared common letters in the same sequence.

While Goswami showed that children can make analogies between words with the same letter sequences, a reanalysis of her findings gives one more indication that children use letter-onset and letter-rime correspondences rather than letter-phoneme correspondences. Although Goswami found children could make analogies between words with the same sequence of letters, she also found the children were significantly better at making analogies between words such as *hark-lark*, where the same letter sequences are at the ends of words, than between words such as *hark-harm*, where the same letter sequences are at the beginnings of words.

What could explain this difference? Notice that the letters *-ark* in *hark* and *lark* represent whole rimes while the letters *har-* in *hark* and *harm* represent an onset, /h/, and a phoneme, /ar/, within the rimes /ark/ and /arm/. Once again children's ability to work with letters representing whole rimes contrasts with their difficulty in working with letters representing phonemes within rimes. Hence, Goswami's data suggest that children can make analogies between familiar and unfamiliar print words to figure out how to say unfamiliar print words when the print words have common letters representing whole rimes. Goswami did another study with Felicity Mead (1992) and together they also found that children make analogies between letter sequences representing rimes significantly better than they make analogies between letter sequences representing phonemes that are parts of rimes.

> Children make analogies between familiar and unfamiliar print words to figure out how to say unfamiliar print words.

My research asked the question, "What better explains children's pronunciation of unfamiliar print words, their knowledge of letter-phoneme correspondences or their knowledge of other print words?" (Moustafa 1990, 1995). To answer this question I asked seventy-five children in their last six weeks of first grade to read aloud a picture book I had rewritten so it consisted of (1) words commonly taught to beginning readers and (2) unusual words. The commonly taught words were *big, black, blue, brown, funny, green, hat, just, little, light, new, old, pretty, red, right, round, small, stop, too,* and *yellow*. The unusual words, either very uncommon words or made-up words, were *blound, bittle, brust, foo, grack, hew, jop, lat, nellow, prust, rue, smed, steen, tunny,* and *yig*. The letters in the unusual words consisted of letters representing onsets plus letters representing rimes in the common words. For example, *rue* consisted of the *r* in *red* and the *ue* in *blue*. Similarly *grack* consisted of the *gr-* in *green* and the *-ack* in *black*. I also showed each child the letters and digraphs (such as *r* and *ue*) that represented the phonemes in the unusual words and asked them to tell me the sounds of the letters.

Figure 5.2 shows my findings. I found that the children's knowledge of the common words accounted for 95 percent of the unusual words they were able to say correctly. That is, if the children could pronounce *rue*, they almost always could pronounce both *red* and *blue*. Similarly, if they could say *grack*, they almost always could say both *green* and *black*.

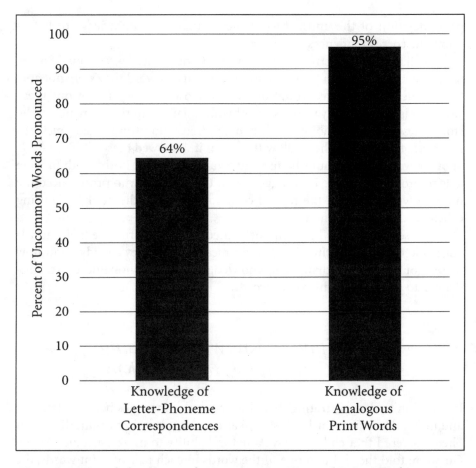

*Figure 5.2 Knowledge Sources for Pronouncing Unusual Print Words*

While the children's knowledge of the common words accounted for 95 percent of the unusual words they were able to pronounce, the children's knowledge of letter-phoneme correspondences accounted for only 64 percent of the unusual words they were able to pronounce. That is, 36 percent of the time the children were able to correctly identify an unusual word, they could not correctly identify the sounds of all the letters and digraphs that constituted the word. For example, many children who correctly pronounced *rue* also correctly pronounced both *red* and *blue* but told me that *r* was /r/, and *ue* was /u/ and /e/.

When we compare theories in science, the theory that best accounts for the facts is considered the more viable. In this experiment, the children's knowledge of words they already recognized accounted for their pronunciation of the unusual words better than their knowledge of letter-phoneme correspondences.

A theory is even stronger if it can account for its "exceptions." Sometimes when the children were able to say an unusual word they were not able to say one of the related common words. How did they figure out these words? It is possible they were using other familiar words that were not in the story. I tested this possibility with two children who pronounced *grack* but not *black*, the word in the book with *-ack* in it. I showed these children *back*, another word which could be used to figure out *grack*. Both children were able to pronounce *back*. This suggests that the children who pronounced the unusual words but not the related common words in the book were using other words that they knew.

These research findings support a theory that children use their knowledge of letters representing onsets and rimes in words they already know how to pronounce, rather than their knowledge of letter-phoneme correspondences, to pronounce unfamiliar words.

## *Multiplying Knowledge: Using What One Knows to Know More*

In addition to demonstrating that children make analogies between familiar and unfamiliar print words, Goswami also made a very important discovery. She discovered that children have a natural ability to make analogies. When Goswami told the children one of the words in each pair of print words, the kindergarten-age children were able to figure out the unfamiliar analogous print word as often as the second-grade-age children. Similarly, the children at the lowest reading level were able to figure out the unfamiliar analogous words as often as the children at the more advanced reading levels. Hence, Goswami concluded that children have the ability to make analogies at all ages and at all reading levels.

Goswami suggested that what changes as children become more proficient readers is not children's ability to make analogies but the number of print words that they recognize. That is, as children learn to recognize more and more print words they have more print words they can use to figure out unfamiliar print words.

Goswami's suggestion is supported by my own findings. Figure 5.3 shows the number of common words and the number of unusual words each child was able to pronounce when he or she read the book in my experiment.

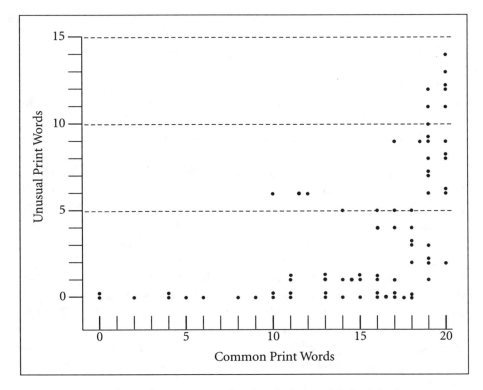

*Figure 5.3 Numbers of Common and Related Unusual Print Words Pronounced by Children*

In the figure each dot represents a child. To see how many common words a particular child read, look at the numbers on the horizontal line directly below the dot. To see how many unusual words that same child read, look at the numbers on the vertical line to the left of the dot. For example, the two children represented by the two dots in the lower, left-hand corner of the figure were not able to read any common words or any unusual words. The child represented by the dot in the upper, right-hand corner of the figure read 20 common words and 14 unusual words.

As Figure 5.3 shows, no child converted any of the unusual words into spoken words unless he or she already knew a lot of the common words in the experiment. Furthermore, every child who knew most of the common words in the experiment was able to pronounce at least one unusual word. In short, the more print words the children knew how to pronounce, the more unfamiliar words they were able to figure out how to pronounce.

Put another way, children need to learn to recognize a lot of print words before they begin to make analogies between familiar and unfamiliar print words. When children have enough print words they recognize, they will make analogies between familiar and unfamiliar print words. How much is enough? This will vary from child to child, of course. The important point is, this is the process children use to figure out unfamiliar print words.[5] Some children will figure out how to do it before other children, but all children who learn to recognize lots of print words holistically will eventually figure it out.

Some may doubt that children really will make analogies without direct, explicit instruction. One particularly good piece of evidence that children will learn letter-onset and letter-rime correspondences without direct instruction is a study done by William Tunmer and Andrew Nesdale (1985). Tunmer and Nesdale were interested in establishing the necessity of instructing children in letter-phoneme correspondences. They studied six first-grade classes. In three of the classes the teachers emphasized instruction in letter-phoneme correspondences and using letter-phoneme correspondences to pronounce words. In the other three classes the teachers ignored letter-phoneme instruction. At the end of the school year Tunmer and Nesdale asked the children in the six classes to pronounce real print words and print words they had made up by changing one letter in the real words.

Tunmer and Nesdale found whether or not the children had received instruction in letter-phoneme correspondences made very little difference in how many of the made-up print words the children were able to figure out. However, they found that the number of real print words the children could figure out did make a difference in the number of made-up print words they could figure out. Those who could not pronounce many real print words could not pronounce many made-up print words. Those who could pronounce a large number of real print words could pronounce a large number of made-up print words.[6] In short, instruction in letter-phoneme correspon-

---

[5]This mental process is similar to the process linguists have discovered children use to acquire productive oral language. See Moustafa (1990, pp. 42–45) for a discussion on the similarity.

[6]Tunmer and Nesdale drew different conclusions from their data. Although they found a low correlation between pseudoword recoding and phonemic awareness, they assume that phonemic awareness is essential to productive recoding. This is an *a priori* interpretation, not a data-driven one.

dences did not make the difference in how many words the children could figure out; the number of print words the children could recognize made the difference.

## *Recapping the Research Findings on Acquiring Letter-Sound Correspondences*

What does this mean? First, it means that now we have unlocked the secret of how children make letter-sound correspondences. Rather than learning letter-phoneme correspondences as we adults have traditionally assumed children must do, children actually use letter-rime and letter-onset correspondences. It also means we have now unlocked the secret of how children use letter-sound correspondences to figure out how to pronounce new print words. Rather than using letter-phoneme rules taught to them by someone else, they use letter-onset and letter-rime correspondences in print words they already know to figure out how to pronounce new print words with the same letter sequences. Finally, it means that this process is a spontaneous process, one that children do quite naturally, not as a prerequisite to learning to make sense of print, but as a consequence of learning to make sense of print.

> Rather than using letter-phoneme rules taught to them by someone else, children use letter-onset and letter-rime correspondences in print words they already know to figure out how to pronounce new print words with the same letter sequences.

For example, through shared reading with predictable stories children might learn to recognize the words *small* and *smile* and figure out that *sm-* is pronounced /sm/. Similarly they might learn to recognize *cart* and *part* and figure out that *-art* is /art/. Then when they encounter *smart* they can use their knowledge of the *sm-* in *small* and *smile* and the *-art* in *cart* and *part* to pronounce *smart*.

# Applying the Research Findings: Helping Children Use Their Knowledge of Spoken Sounds to Pronounce Unfamiliar Print

I can think of at least three conclusions that might be drawn from the information in this chapter: (1) we should teach children to make analogies between familiar and unfamiliar print words so they can pronounce unfamiliar print words; (2) we should teach children the sounds of letters that represent onsets and rimes so they can pronounce unfamiliar print words; (3) we should teach children to recognize lots of print words holistically so they can make analogies between familiar and unfamiliar print words to pronounce unfamiliar print words. Let's examine these ideas, one by one.

How about the first idea, teaching children to make analogies between familiar and unfamiliar print words? This is a new idea, but an unnecessary one. Goswami found that children have a natural ability to make analogies. What develops is *not* children's ability to make analogies but the number of print words they recognize that serve as the basis for making analogies. Allegorically speaking, if we are caring for malnourished children, should we give them instructions on how to digest food, or should we give them food to digest?

How about the second and third ideas? For both of them, it very much depends on whether they are taught *in* context or *out* of context.

If the second idea, teaching children the sounds of letters that represent onsets and rimes, is done outside of a meaningful context, it is just a modern version of the age-old letter-emphasis approach. Just as letters representing phonemes are nonsense outside of context, letters representing onsets and rimes are also nonsense outside of context, and we all have trouble remembering nonsense. In Chapter 3, we reviewed research that demonstrated that early readers read words in context better than out of context. Teaching children the sounds of letters representing onsets and rimes on lists or cards robs children of the chance to use their knowledge of language and the world to figure out print words.

Moreover, teaching early readers parts of words outside of a meaningful context conveys an erroneous message about what reading is. As you know, children have a marvelous capacity to pick up on what we do rather than what we tell them to do. If we tell children that reading is meaning*ful* but teach them to read using meaning*less* activities (for example, "circle the words that have an /ok/ sound"), we are giving them an implicit but powerful message that reading is a meaningless activity. If we teach them to read using meaningful materials, we give them an implicit but powerful message that reading is a meaningful activity.

However, if teaching the sounds of letters representing onsets and rimes is done *in* context, it can help early readers remember letter-sound correspondences. For example, I once had the opportunity to live in a country where public signs are in Arabic. In Arabic, the letters used to represent *f* and *k* are identical except one has one dot above it and the other has two dots above it. When I was taught these Arabic letters one-by-one in isolation, I had trouble remembering which was which. Then one day, driving down a street, my husband (who reads Arabic) pointed to a red octagon-shaped sign at an intersection and said "kif," the Arabic word for *stop*. Since then, I've been able to remember which Arabic letter has one dot and which has two—I only have to think about Arabic stop signs, and I know.

The reason this experience helped me remember which letter was which was that the letters were written in an environmental context. However, only a small number of the words that children need to recognize to become independent readers are in such contexts. How, you might ask, can we teach early readers letter-sound correspondences in the context of words if early readers have difficulty remembering words out of context? This is a puzzle that I will return to in the last chapter of this book. In the meantime, let's look at the third idea, teaching children to recognize lots of print words so they can make analogies among familiar and unfamiliar print words.

Up to this point, we have looked at studies that involve print words presented in isolation or uncommon or made up words in a story context. These studies enable us to figure out how children make letter-sound correspondences. This is a researcher's way of studying phonomena. However, it is not the way real reading (in other words, making sense of print) occurs.

In Chapter 3 we reviewed research that demonstrates that children are better able to recognize words in context than in isolation. When words are in isolation, as in word lists or on word cards, children are deprived of contextual and linguistic cues. However, when words are in a context, such as the context of a story, children can use their knowledge of the world and their knowledge of language to help them figure out unfamiliar print words. Recall that in Chapter 3 when you recognized some print words in the passage with the blanks, you were able to figure out the words that belonged in the blanks without seeing any letters. Recall also how difficult it was for you to identify the "word" !-% in Chapter 3 when I asked, "What is the 'word' !-%?" It was much easier for you when you went back to the passage and used your knowledge of English to figure it out.

What happens when children are able to use both context and letter-sound correspondences to figure out print words? In another experiment, Goswami (1988) studied the ability of six- and seven-year-old children who had begun to read to use analogy with real, meaningful print words while reading a story. Before she met with the children she wrote a short story entitled "Hark! and Listen!" In the story there were six words with the same letter sequences as *hark*: *bark, dark, lark* and *hard, harm, harp*. Based on Goswami's 1986 study where she showed children two words side by side and told the children one of the words, we would expect that *hard, harm*, and *harp* would be more difficult than *bark, dark*, and *lark* since the letters *-ark* in *hark, bark, dark*, and *lark* represent a rime while the letters *har-* in *hark, hard, harm*, and *harp* represent a single-phoneme onset, /h/, and phonemes, /ar/, within a rime.

Goswami met with the children, one by one. First she found out which print words they already knew how to convert into spoken language. Then, she showed each child the title of the passage and taught each child to read *hark*. Finally, she asked each child to read the passage.

Goswami found when the children read the words in the context of a story, it was no more difficult for the children to make analogies between *hark* and *hard, harm*, and *harp* (words that share an onset and phonemes within a rime) than to make analogies between *hark* and *bark, dark*, and *lark* (words that share whole rimes). Once again, Goodman's explanation rings true: "In lists children had only cues within printed words while in stories they had additional cues in the flow of the language" to help them figure out new print words. In the story the children were able to use both context and letter-sound correspondences in familiar words to figure out unfamiliar words. Under these circumstances the children did better than expected when they had had only "cues within words." Put another way, when the children were encountering unfamiliar print words in a meaningful story, as opposed to words in a list, they were able to play with a full deck.

In Chapter 3 we saw that even though English is written alphabetically, it doesn't have to be read sound by sound. English, like the Chinese logographic writing system, can be read holistically. If we teach children to recognize print words holistically in stories with a natural flow of language through instructional strategies such as shared reading—rather than teaching them word parts or words in isolation—we would be providing them with the optimum way of acquiring a large number of print words. At first children will use their knowledge of language and their knowledge of the world to help them learn to recognize a lot of print words holistically. This process is facilitated by instructional strategies such as shared reading with predictable stories. Then, as children acquire more and more print words that they recognize holistically, they will also use their natural ability to make analogies between familiar and unfamiliar print words to figure out how to pronounce even more unfamiliar print words. Eventually, after a great deal of experience with reading, they will be able to pronounce unfamiliar print words out of context as we very experienced readers can (but seldom) do. Hence, teaching children to recognize lots of print words holistically when that teaching is done in the context of continuous text with language familiar to children is a powerful precursor to independent reading. In Chapter 8 I will describe a way to teach letter-onset and letter-rime correspondences in the context of stories which builds on children's natural learning processes.

> As children learn to recognize more and more print words in context, their natural ability to make analogies between familiar and unfamiliar print words will help them figure out how to pronounce unfamiliar print words by themselves.

Now we can explain the findings of the studies I reported on in Chapter 3, the studies by the NAEP, Ribowsky, Reutzel and Cooter, Freepon, Feitelson and her colleagues, Richek and McTague, and Elley, where children who were learning to read stories with familiar language became better able to pronounce unfamiliar print than those who were receiving traditional phonics instruction. They were better at pronouncing unfamiliar print because they were reading, or being helped to read, stories with familiar language. As they learned to recognize more and more print words in the context of familiar language, they were better able to figure out how to pronounce print words they had never seen before. The surprising, counterintuitive finding of research is that less traditional phonics instruction is actually better than more, provided children are being helped to read stories with language that is familiar to them.

In summary, the optimum way to help children use their knowledge of spoken sounds to figure out unfamiliar print words is to help them learn to recognize print words in context. If we show children print words holistically in a natural context, such as in a story, we will be providing contextual and linguistic support to help them remember the print words. Then, as children learn to recognize more and more print words in context, their natural ability to use language to figure out unfamiliar print words and their natural ability to make analogies between familiar and unfamiliar print words will help them to figure out how to pronounce even more unfamiliar print words by themselves. Such an approach underscores the fact that reading is a meaningful activity.

If children are pronouncing print but do not understand what they are saying, they are *not* reading. As my study and Tunmer and Nesdale's study with uncommon and made-up words illustrate (and as experienced teachers know all too well), once children learn how to recognize some print words they can become quite capable of pronouncing other print words without understanding the meaning of what they are saying.

Reading is not pronouncing print but making sense of print. So far we have discussed how children learn to pronounce unfamiliar print, but we have not yet discussed how children make sense of print. That is the topic of the next chapter.

# 6

# How Children Use Their Knowledge of the World to Make Sense of Print

IN MY FIRST TEACHING ASSIGNMENT MANY YEARS AGO, I HAD A
small group of fourth-grade children who needed reading materials beyond
those available in the school's reading program. Responding to their need, a
parent (and school board member) gave me a set of small, beautifully illus-
trated books about the (then) new American astronaut program. Delighted
to have the books, I sat down with the children and listened as they took
turns reading the books to me. They read the story so well. Their intonation
was so natural, their voices rising and falling just where they should. I was so
proud of them. Then I asked them what the story was about. One after the
other, they shyly shrugged their shoulders and said, "I don't know."

The children were converting print into spoken language, but they were
not making sense of print. Why weren't the children making sense of print?
Schema theory helps us understand what was happening. In the following
pages I will explain schema theory and how our schemas affect our ability to
make sense of print. Then I will return to this incident with my fourth-grade
students. By way of illustration I will begin by summarizing schema research
on adults. Then I will go on to discuss schema research on children.

## How We Adults Use Our Knowledge
## of the World to Make Sense of Print

We are all aware of what we get *from* reading—ideas, information, enjoyment, and excitement. Something we are usually not aware of, if everything

goes well, is what we bring *to* reading to make sense of print. For example, read the following passage:

> John checked in at the doctor's office. He was given some forms. A few minutes later, he was escorted to an examination room and given a gown. The doctor examined John and wrote a prescription. When John was finished, he paid the bill and left.

Cover the passage and don't look back. Now answer the following questions. Who gave John the forms? Who escorted John to the examination room?

Now look back at the passage and find where it says who gave John the forms. Find where it says who escorted John to the examination room.

The point is, not everything you understood when you read the passage was actually written in the passage. In making sense of the passage, you were drawing on information that was not in the passage. Just as you used your knowledge about cowboys to make sense of the cowboy sentence in Chapter 3, here you used your background knowledge about visiting doctors' offices, or your knowledge of the world, to make sense of this passage.

A term that means the same thing as background knowledge, or knowledge of the world, is *schema*.[1] Although the term was first used by Sir Frederick Bartlett in 1932, schema theory has largely developed since Flesch wrote *Why Johnny Can't Read*.

Each of us has schemas for many things that we have developed over our years of living. We have schemas for restaurants, zoos, gardening, mystery movies, traveling, forests, and so on. For each of us, our schemas on some topics are more developed than those on other topics, depending on our experiences and interests. A person living in an arctic climate will have a highly developed schema for snowy terrains and snowstorms while another person living in a hot, dry climate will have a highly developed schema for desert terrains and sandstorms.

According to schema theory, when we read a passage, we first locate the relevant schema in our memories. In the cowboy sentence in Chapter 3, the second word, *cowboy*, helped you to use your knowledge about cowboys. In the doctor's office passage, the words *checked in* and *doctor's office* helped you to use your knowledge about a doctor's office.

The following passage by John Bransford and Marcia Johnson (1972) is

---

[1]The plural of schema is schemata but I will use the Anglicized version, schemas.

one of the best-known passages used in schema-theory research. Take a minute to read it through once. Then I'll ask you questions.

> The procedure is actually quite simple. First you arrange things into different groups. Of course, one pile may be sufficient depending on how much there is to do. If you have to go somewhere else due to a lack of facilities that is the next step, otherwise you are pretty well set. It is important not to overdo things. That is, it is better to do too few things at once than too many. In the short run this may not seem important but complications can easily arise. A mistake can be expensive as well. At first the whole procedure will seem complicated. Soon, however, it will become just another facet of life. It is difficult to foresee any end to the necessity for this task in the immediate future, but then one never can tell. After the procedure is completed one arranges the materials into different groups again. Then they can be put into their appropriate places. Eventually they will be used once more and the whole cycle will then have to be repeated. However, that is part of life.

Without looking back, write down what the passage was all about. Jot down the big idea and then as many details as you can remember.

Many people who read this passage have difficulty making sense of it—until they are told that the passage is about washing clothes. If you didn't realize that it was about washing clothes when you read it, read it again and see if it makes more sense to you now.

Now stop and jot down the big idea and as many details as you can remember. Did you remember more things? Did the passage make more sense this time?

The point of the washing clothes passage is to illustrate how locating an appropriate schema helps us make sense of written messages. Locating a schema before one reads a passage is necessary to make sense of it. However, locating a schema after we read a passage does not help us make sense of it. Bransford and Johnson gave the washing clothes passage to three groups of people: one group was told what the passage was about before they read it, one group was told what the passage was about after they read it, and one group was not told what the passage was about at all. The people who were told what the passage was about before they read it comprehended and recalled the passage significantly better than the other two groups.

Try the experiment yourself. Have some of your friends read the washing clothes passage but don't tell them what the passage is about. After they have read the passage, ask them to explain to you as much as they can. Then, tell some other friends what the passage is about and ask them to read it. After they have read it, ask them to explain to you as much as they can. See which group of friends makes more sense of the passage.

Once we have located a schema that fits the passage, our schema does several things for us. First it helps us interpret the rest of the passage. For example, read the following two sentences by David Rumelhart (1985):

> The statistician could be certain that the difference was significant since all the figures on the right hand side of the table were larger than any of those on the left.

> The craftsman was certainly justified in charging more for the carvings on the right since all the figures on the right hand side of the table were larger than any of those on the left.

Both sentences have the phrase *since all the figures on the right hand side of the table were larger than any of those on the left.* However, the words *figures* and *table* have different meanings in the two different contexts. Probably you weren't even aware of the different meanings of *figures* and *table* when you read the first sentence. You had already located your mathematical schema. Consequently, you didn't need a figurine schema. As a matter of fact, the washing clothes passage above can be read another way. Try reading it as if a bureaucrat is sorting papers. You can still make sense of it, but a very different sense, without one word in the passage being changed.

The better developed our schemas on a topic, the better we can make sense of and recall what we have read. George Spilich, Gregg Vesonder, Harry Chiesi, and James Voss (1979) gave a passage about baseball to people who already knew a great deal about baseball and people who had little knowledge of baseball. They found differences in both the quantity and the quality of what each group recalled. Those who knew a lot about baseball remembered the passage much better than those who knew less about baseball. They also recalled much more that was relevant to the passage than those who knew less about baseball.

Finally, our schemas facilitate our reading. That is the reason it was not necessary for you to see all the letters—or even all the words—when you read the cowboy sentence.

Of course, sometimes we locate a schema other than the one intended by the writer. If we do, something in the passage may signal that we are misinterpreting the passage and then we select another schema. You will notice when you do this that you spontaneously go back to the point where you think your misunderstanding began and read the part you misunderstood again.

A schema we all use when we read is our schema for language—in our case, when reading and writing this book, the English language. For example, read the following sentence:

> If you didn't realize that it was about washing clothes when you read it, read it again.

The print word *read* occurred twice in this sentence. The first time you encountered *read* you pronounced it one way. The second time you pronounced it another way. Why did you do that? Both words were written exactly alike. There was nothing in the words themselves to signal the different pronunciations.

The print word *read* is one of a special group of print words called *homographs*. Homographs are print words whose pronunciations vary with their meanings. They are a good example of how our knowledge of spoken language helps us interpret print. In the following pairs of sentences I have italicized the homographs. Notice how they take on different meanings and pronunciations with different contexts.

> They *live* in New York. / They broadcast *live* from New York.
> *Does* it look beautiful? / The *does* are beautiful.
> He broke the *record*. / Did he *record* the grades?

How did you know how to pronounce the italicized words in each of these sentences? You used your knowledge of English, or, in Goodman's words, "the flow of the language," to help you interpret the print. What Goodman referred to as readers using "the flow of the language" in 1965 is now referred to by many researchers as our "schema for language."

Using our schemas for language and the world to interpret information is not unique to reading. We also use our schemas to interpret what we hear. In another experiment with the washing clothes passage Bransford and Johnson (1972) had people listen to a tape recording of the passage. Again, those who were told what the passage was about before they heard the passage understood and remembered it significantly better than both those who were told what the passage was about after they heard it and those who were not told what it was about at all. Similarly, Chiesi, Spilich, and Voss (1979) asked people to listen to a tape recording about baseball and found those who knew more about baseball recalled significantly more of what they heard than those who knew less about baseball.

Just as we occasionally select a schema other than the one intended by the writer when we are reading, we also occasionally select a schema other than the one intended by the speaker when we are listening. All of us have experienced a conversation in which we initially misunderstood the other person and then, when the misunderstanding became apparent, said, "Oh, I thought you meant. . . !"

Our schemas help us not only to understand what we read and what we hear, but also to function in life. Imagine trying to drive a car if you had never seen a car before, or understanding a street map if you had never left your home—or reading this book if you didn't know that reading is a meaningful activity.

## How Children Use Their Knowledge of the World to Make Sense of Spoken Messages

Children, like adults, use schema to help them function in life.[2] Without schemas they would not be able to find a ball that had gone behind a fence. Without schemas they would not be able to walk from the bedroom to the kitchen, from the bus stop to the classroom.

Several experiments demonstrate that children use their schemas to make sense of what they hear. Drew Arnold and Penelope Brooks (1976) did an experiment, similar to Bransford and Johnson's washing clothes experiment, with second- and fifth-grade children, where the children listened to ambiguous passages. Like the washing clothes passage, the messages in the passages were ambiguous but could be made clear by a picture or an explanation.

Arnold and Brooks found that the children better recalled what they had heard and made better inferences when they were told what an ambiguous passage was about before they heard the passage than when they were not told what an ambiguous passage was about. The experiment demonstrates that children, like adults, must locate relevant schema to make sense of what they hear.

---

[2]See Piaget's pioneering work on schema development in children, summarized in Ginsburg and Opper (1979).

Another study demonstrated that the background knowledge children bring to what they hear affects their understanding of what they hear. Ann Brown, Sandra Smiley, Jeanne Day, Michael Townsend, and Sallie Lawton (1977) had second-, fourth-, and sixth-grade children listen to a story invented by the researchers about a fictitious Targa tribe. Before the children listened to the story, Brown and her colleagues led one group of children to think that the Targas were an Eskimo tribe by showing them pictures of the Targa people in a cold, wintery environment. They led a second group of children to think that the Targas were desert Native Americans by showing them pictures of the Targa people in a hot, dry climate. They didn't tell a third group of children anything about the Targas.

Brown and her colleagues found that the first two groups of children interpreted the passage according to the background information they had been given. The children who thought the Targas were Eskimos interpreted the reference to "extreme temperatures" in the passage as a reference to very cold temperatures. The children who thought the Targas were desert Native Americans interpreted the reference to "extreme temperatures" as a reference to very hot temperatures.

Brown and her associates also found that the children who were given background information about the Targas before they heard the passage recalled much more of what they heard than the children who were not given background information about the Targas before they heard the passage. They found this was true regardless of the age of the children in the study: the youngest children in the study were just as dependent on their schema to make sense of a passage as the oldest children. Indeed, they concluded that children show the same basic patterns as adults in needing and using schema.

What does change as children become older, Brown and her colleagues found, is not the process of comprehending but the number of ideas in the passage children are able to recall. The older children recalled more than the younger children. What could account for this finding?

Chiesi, Spilich, and Voss's experiment that found that those with more developed schemas on baseball remembered more of what they heard when they listened to the tape recorded passage on baseball suggests that the older children in the study were able to recall more than the younger children because they had more developed schemas on deserts, the arctic climate, hunting, and so on. Hence, it appears that what changes as children grow older is not their need and ability to use schema to comprehend, but the degree to which their schemas are developed on particular topics. The degree to which their schemas are developed on particular topics would reflect their life experiences and education.

# How Children Use Their Knowledge of the World to Make Sense of Print

If children use their schemas to make sense of what they hear, we would expect them to use their schemas to make sense of what they read. The research shows not only that children use their schemas to make sense of print but also that the amount of background knowledge children have on a topic prior to reading a passage has a powerful effect on their abilities to make sense of the passage.

---

The amount of background knowledge children have on a topic prior to reading a passage has a powerful effect on their abilities to make sense of the passage.

---

In an experiment similar to the one using the baseball passage, David Pearson, Jane Hansen, and Christine Gordon (1979) did an experiment with second-grade children using a passage on spiders. The children were average-ability second-graders with the same overall intelligence and general reading level. First they gave the children a test to see how much they knew about spiders. Then they asked the children to read a passage on spiders. After the children read the passage they asked them questions about the passage. They found that the children who knew more about spiders before they read the passage were much better at answering questions on implicit information in the passage than the children who knew less about spiders before they read the passage.

What if the children in this study who knew less about spiders happened to know more about another topic? Would they still be poorer readers? And what if the children who knew more about spiders knew less about the other topic? Would they still be better readers? Several studies address this question.

In one study Barbara Taylor (1979) gave third- and fifth-grade children passages on a topic generally familiar to children—bird nest building—and on a topic generally unfamiliar to children—bee dancing. The third-grade children were average third-grade readers. Some of the fifth-grade children were average fifth-grade readers and some were below average. Taylor asked each child, one by one, to read the passages silently and then retell the story orally. The children gave better retellings of the familiar topic than of the unfamiliar topic. Figure 6.1 illustrates how each group of children did on the retellings of the passages on familiar and unfamiliar topics. The third-grade readers went from an average retelling score of 10 points on the unfamiliar topic to an average retelling score of 14 points on the familiar topic. The average fifth-grade readers went from an average retelling score of 19 points on the unfamiliar topic to an average retelling score of 23

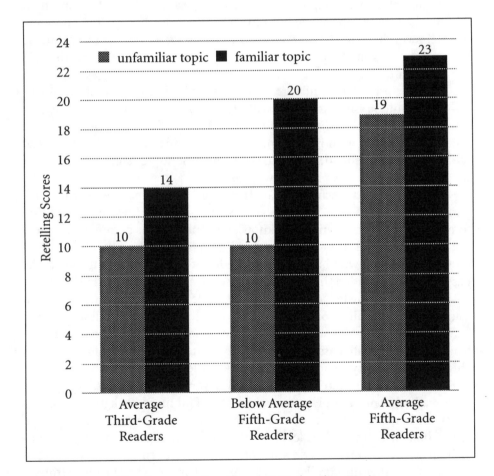

*Figure 6.1 Retelling Scores on Familiar and Unfamiliar Topics*

points on the familiar topic. The below-average fifth-grade readers were the most affected by whether they were reading on a familiar or unfamiliar topic. They went from an average retelling score of 10 points on the unfamiliar topic to an average retelling score of 20 points on the familiar topic.

In another study, Marjorie Lipson (1983) gave fourth-, fifth-, and sixth-grade Catholic children attending a Catholic school and fourth-, fifth-, and sixth-grade Jewish children attending a Hebrew school two reading passages; one was entitled *First Communion* and the other was entitled *Bar Mitzvah*. All the children were average and above-average readers. Lipson found the children attending the Catholic school read faster, recalled more, made fewer errors, and made better inferences in the passage about the first communion than in the passage about the bar mitzvah. Similarly, the children attending the Hebrew school read faster, recalled more, made fewer errors, and made better inferences in the passage about the bar mitzvah than about the first communion.

Other studies had similar results. Mary Beth Marr and Kathleen Gormley (1982) did a similar study with fourth-grade children and Theresa Roberts (1988) did a similar study with fifth- and ninth-grade children. Again, the children with more knowledge on specific topics before they read the passage comprehended the passages on those topics significantly better than did those with less prior knowledge.

Finally, Donna Recht and Lauren Leslie (1988) replicated the baseball passage experiment with seventh- and eighth-graders. However, in addition to measuring the children's prior knowledge on the topic before giving them the passage to read, they also measured their general reading ability. They found the children who had more knowledge of baseball before they read the passage comprehended the passage on baseball significantly better than those with less prior knowledge of baseball, regardless of whether they had been classified as low-ability or high-ability readers. That is, the children with a "low reading ability" who had more prior knowledge of baseball comprehended the baseball passage significantly better than the children with a "high reading ability" who had less prior knowledge of baseball.

Hence, the children in all these studies were "better readers" when they were reading about a topic about which they had more background knowledge—or better-developed schemas—than when they were reading about a topic about which they had less background knowledge. These experiments explain why my fourth-grade students who were such good readers when they were reading on familiar topics could not make sense of the astronaut story: they lacked the background knowledge to comprehend the story. For children, as for adults, comprehension during reading is a result of the background knowledge they bring to reading. The more background knowledge children have on a topic prior to reading a passage on that topic, the more they are able to make sense of the passage.

## How Children Use Their Knowledge of Language to Make Sense of Print

Just as children use their schemas on particular topics (e.g., spiders, bird nest building, baseball, soccer, religious rites, etc.) to make sense of print, they—like us—also use their schema for the particular language they speak to make sense of print. This is, in fact, what Goodman demonstrated when he showed that children can read words better in stories than in lists. It is also what Rhodes and what Kucer demonstrated when they gave children text where the flow of the language was kept natural and text where the flow of the language was distorted and found that the children were better able to comprehend the texts with natural language.

While Goodman, Rhodes, and Kucer looked at natural language versus contrived language, Robert Ruddell (1965) looked at two types of natural language: (1) natural language where the flow of the language is typical of children's spoken language and (2) natural language where the flow of the language is typical of written language, but *not* children's spoken language. Ruddell wrote six reading passages, three where the flow of the language was typical of fourth-grade children's spoken language (e.g., "A spaceman could fix the small hole") and three where the flow of the language was not typical of fourth-grade children's spoken language (e.g., "The leader gave the men short breaks because they needed rest"). He asked fourth-grade children to read the passages. He found the children were able to comprehend the passages where the flow of the language was typical of their spoken language much better than the passages where the flow of the language was not typical of their spoken language.

Susan Tatham (1970) did a similar study with second- and fourth-grade children using sentences rather than passages. Like Ruddell, she found that the children comprehended sentences where the flow of the language was typical of their spoken language significantly better than sentences where the flow of the language was not typical of their spoken language.

In addition to helping children comprehend reading passages, children's schema for the particular language they speak also helps them pronounce homographs, words like *read, live, does, record,* and many other words whose pronunciations vary with their meanings. Homographs are another reason for teaching children to read words in context rather than in isolation. Context helps readers figure out familiar print words as well as unfamiliar print words.

## Helping Children Develop Their Knowledge of the World

If background knowledge has such a powerful influence on children's ability to make sense of print, how can we help children develop their background knowledge? There are several ways.

One way—one that we do quite naturally long before reading instruction begins in school—is to provide children with a variety of interesting experiences. As we take young children to the store, zoo, airport, beach, auto repair shop, and on vacations, and talk with them about our shared experiences and about other things and events that interest them, we help them acquire background knowledge about various places and events and language associated with these places and events.

Another way to help children build their background knowledge is to provide them with books, TV programs, videos, and movies that expand their knowledge of the world. Young children can vicariously visit historical Europe through *Cinderella* and travelogues of castles. Urban children can vicariously learn about forests through *Bambi* and nature movies and videos. Older children may "live" historical events through historical novels and historical movies and videos such as *Gone with the Wind*. Again, as they acquire concepts, they acquire language associated with the concepts.

Still another way we can help children comprehend text on an unfamiliar topic is to provide them with background information on that topic before they read on the topic. Kathleen Stevens (1982) gave high school students a reading passage about a battle in the Texan War. She found that the students who were given background information about the Texan War before they read the passage were significantly better able to understand the passage than students who were not given background information before they read the passage.

Similarly, Isabel Beck, Richard Omanson, and Margaret McKeown (1982) gave third-graders background knowledge they needed to comprehend a story about a raccoon. (See also Omanson, Beck, Voss, and McKeown 1984.) They found that children who had the background information about raccoon behavior before they read the story recalled the story significantly better than those who just talked about raccoons in general. Victoria Risko and Marino Alvarez (1986) did a similar study with fourth-, fifth-, and sixth-grade children and reported similar findings.

These studies suggest that my fourth-grade students might have understood the astronaut story if I had immersed them in a science unit on outer space before I gave them the story. (Today, teachers would also be aided by the many news releases on space shuttles and space exploration and by the science fiction TV programs on space travel.)

Finally, another way we can help children build their background knowledge is to provide them with a variety of reading materials on the same topic. Linda Crafton (1983) demonstrated this when she gave high school students reading materials on unfamiliar topics. She gave one group of students two magazine articles on different topics and another group of students two magazine articles on the same topic. She asked all the students to read the articles one after the other. Crafton found reading two different articles on the same topic dramatically improved the students' comprehension of the second article. The students who read on the same topic in the successive readings gave lengthier, more organized, and more focused retellings about their second reading than the students who read on different topics in the successive readings did about their second reading. Moreover, they were more personally involved in the reading than the students who read on different topics. The same-topic group retold many more ideas than the different-topic group. While the retelling scores by the same-topic group ranged from 21 to 99 (out of a possible 100 points) with an average of 66 points, the retelling scores by the different-topic group ranged from 10 to 70 points with an average of 32 points.

When my oldest son was in sixth grade he had an experience similar to the one in Crafton's experiment. He and his classmates were given the last hour of each school day to choose and read books on any topic of their choosing among a large collection of books. My son chose dolphins. He got so much pleasure out of his readings that within a few weeks I found him eagerly reading an article about dolphins in an encyclopedia written for adults. Crafton's findings suggest that my son was able to do this by expanding his knowledge about dolphins as he read multiple articles and books on the same topic.

Can Crafton's strategy be applied to early readers? Yes. Margaret Richek and Becky McTague (1988), who we first met in Chapter 3, reasoned that a connected series of children's books would provide children with conceptually related material. They theorized that as the children moved through each book they would become familiar with characters, plots, and language common to all the books in the series, making each book easier and easier. They tested their hypothesis with second- and third-grade children who were below-average readers for their grades. The series they used was *Curious George*—a series of stories with natural language about a lovable, lively monkey who is always encountering, and being rescued from, mishaps.

At the end of eighteen days (or nine hours) of instruction Richek and McTague tested the children in both their oral reading and comprehension of stories that were *not* in the *Curious George* series. They found that the children in the experiment had improved much more in both their oral reading and comprehension of stories than another group of children of identical age and reading level who had continued with their traditional school curriculum during the same period of time. And all this improvement happened without instruction in letter-sound correspondences.

Just as the background knowledge children have on a topic prior to reading a passage on that topic has a powerful effect on their ability to make sense of the passage, children's background knowledge about print itself has a powerful influence on their ability to learn to read. Children's schema, or background knowledge, for print itself is the topic of the next chapter. It is probably the single most important chapter in this book.

# 7

# How Children Use
# Their Knowledge About
# Reading to Read

WHILE SOME EDUCATORS WERE DEMONSTRATING THAT CHILD-ren use their knowledge of spoken language to figure out unfamiliar print, and other educators were demonstrating that children use their background knowledge to make sense of print, still others began looking beyond the school walls at children's experiences with literacy outside of school. What this third group of educators found has given us a profound insight into how children learn to read.

In this chapter I will first describe findings on children's literacy experiences outside of school in their preschool years. Then I will describe findings on children's literacy experiences outside of school during their school years.

## *Learning About Print*

The first surprise about children's literacy experiences before school was Dolores Durkin's 1961 discovery that some children (approximately 1 percent of the children in the city she studied) learn to read before they are taught to read in school. Durkin found that all the preschool readers she identified had been read to regularly at home and that all of them had at least one person who took the time to answer their questions about reading.

A few years later Don Holdaway and a group of teachers in New Zealand investigated the home backgrounds of proficient young readers (1965, reported in Holdaway 1979). Like Durkin, they found that the children they studied had all been read to at home.

While these findings suggested that reading to children helps children learn to read, the studies lacked a control group, that is, a group of children who were like the children who were read to in all respects except that they had not been read to. Without a control group, we cannot tell if reading to children makes a real difference or if it is just incidental.

---

**Reading to children helps children learn to read.**

---

Although such a control group is needed to establish scientifically that being read to does—or does not—make a difference in how children learn to read, it would be unethical, as well as illegal, to conduct an experiment where we intentionally did not read to children. As we cannot create such a situation experimentally, we would have to find one that occurred naturally.

One such situation occurred in a study conducted in Bristol, England, by a team of researchers led by Gordon Wells (1985, 1986). Wells and his associates observed children from a full range of economic and educational family backgrounds in their homes over a nine-year period—from the time they were fifteen months old until they were ten years old. Wells found a significant relationship between children's knowledge of print when they entered school and their achievement in school. That is, the children who entered school with a relatively greater understanding of print when they were five years old were more likely to enjoy greater academic accomplishments when they were ten years old. On the other hand, the children who entered school with less understanding of print when they were five years old were more likely to have accomplished less academically when they were ten years old.

What would explain this critical difference in children on their entry into school? Why would some children begin school with more understanding of print than others? To answer this question Wells and his colleagues reviewed their records of the children's activities during their preschool years. They looked for occurrences when the children in the study were (1) looking at a picture book and talking about it, (2) listening to a story, (3) drawing and coloring, and (4) writing. Initially, they also looked at instruction in letters as an independent activity, but they found it occurred so rarely that they dropped it from their investigation.

The Bristol study researchers found that of these four literacy-related activities, only one was significantly related to the children's understanding of print when they were five years old: listening to stories. They found that the children with greater understanding of print when they were five had had numerous stories read to them in their preschool years before reading instruction began in school, whereas the children with less understanding of print when they were five had not had as many stories read to them in their preschool years.

Wells suggests that the children who had had more stories read to them before they entered school were better able to learn to read when they went to school. Then, by virtue of being able to read, they were better able to achieve academically. They were able to use reading to learn more.

Wells writes poignantly about one child in the Bristol study who had never had a book read to her in her preschool years, and of her difficulties in learning to read. He contrasts her to another child in the study, who was much more successful academically, who had had over six thousand book and story experiences before starting school.

The Bristol study findings have been replicated again and again. In a study in the U.S., Shirley Brice Heath (1982, 1983) studied adult practices of story reading to preschool children in three neighboring communities. In one community the children tended to do well in reading throughout school. In another community the children tended to do well with workbook pages and other activities characteristic of traditional reading programs in the early elementary school grades, but fell behind in the upper elementary grades. In still another community, the children did poorly in reading throughout school.

Heath found that the adults in each of these communities practiced different story reading to their preschool children. In the community where the children tended to do well in reading throughout school, the parents provided their children with children's books and read stories to them interactively. As they read to them, they made sure their children understood what was being read to them. In the community where the children tended to do well in the early elementary grades but not the later elementary grades, the parents provided their children with children's books, taught them some aspects of traditional literacy instruction, such as the names of the letters, and read them stories. However, when they read stories to their children, they did not interact with their children and did not ensure their children's active involvement in story reading. Rather, they expected their children to sit still and listen as they read to them. Finally, in the community where the children tended to do poorly in reading in school, the parents valued school and saw it as a means of economic advancement for their children. However, they did not provide their preschool children with children's books and they did not read stories to them.

In a study in Israel, Dina Feitelson and Zahava Goldstein (1986) studied kindergartners' home environments in neighborhoods where children tended to do well in school and in neighborhoods where children tended not to do as well. They found that in areas where children tended to do well in school, 96 percent of the children were read to daily and 45 percent of these children were read to for half an hour or more a day. In contrast, they found that in areas where the children tended to do poorly in school, 61 percent of the children were not read to at all. Similarly, they found that in areas where children tended to do well in school, almost half the children were read to regularly before they were two years old. In contrast, in areas where children tended to do poorly in school, none of the children were read to until they were four years old.

In the United States, LaVergne Rosow (1988) interviewed eight adults who were enrolled in literacy programs. She asked them about their past experiences with literacy. Among other things, she found that none of them could recall ever hearing stories or being read to at school or in their homes as they were growing up.

But why should reading stories to children have such a powerful effect on their learning to read? Wells explains that by having stories read to them, children have an opportunity to discover the pleasures and purposes of print. Wells suggests that teaching a child to read before the child understands that reading is a meaningful activity is analogous to teaching a child the rules of his or her language before the child has discovered that language is communication.

> Reading to children helps them discover the pleasures and purposes of print.

An analogy Wells might have made is that teaching children to read before they have discovered the pleasures and purposes of reading would be similar to teaching children to drive before they had discovered the pleasures and purposes of traveling by car. Reading to children before they can read for themselves is similar to allowing children to be passengers in a car before they learn to drive. Reading to children enables them to experience, understand, and appreciate reading.

Wells points out that reading to children also helps them acquire the language of print. This in turn helps them make sense of print. What does

Wells mean by the language of print? Written language differs from spoken language. For example, letters begin with *Dear Johnny* or *Dear Mrs. Smith* and end with *Love* or *Sincerely yours*. A face-to-face greeting might begin with "Hello," "Hi," or "How are you?" and end with "See you," "Bye," or "So long." Fairy tales begin with *Once upon a time* and end with *happily ever after.* A story in face-to-face conversation might begin with "Guess what happened . . ." or "Did you hear about . . ." and end with a listener response.

> Reading to children also helps them acquire the language of print.

The parts between the beginnings and the ends also differ in written and spoken language. Written language usually consists of a series of complete sentences. Spoken language usually consists of turn taking, interruptions, and incomplete sentences in response to questions. Written language uses words like *difficult, repair,* and *cruel.* Spoken language uses words like *hard, fix,* and *mean.* Written language uses phrases like *It is big* and *It has gone.* Spoken language uses phrases like *It's big* and *It's gone.* Written language uses sentences like *The leader gave the men short breaks because they needed rest.* Spoken language uses sentences more like *He called the old woman* and *A spaceman could fix the small hole.*

The findings of other researchers support Wells's explanation that reading to children helps them acquire the language of print. Elizabeth Sulzby (1985) asked children two to five years old who were not yet independent readers to read, or pretend to read, stories. She found that, at first, the children in her study used language similar to their spoken language and what they said did not tell a story across pages. That is, what the children said on each page was about that particular page but not part of a total story. Then, as the children progressed in their development, they increasingly used language typical of written stories and what they said told a story across pages. Since these children were not independent readers we have to assume that they learned the language of print from others reading to them.

Victoria Purcell-Gates (1988) studied kindergarten children who had been read to extensively for two years before starting kindergarten. She asked the children to tell her about their last birthday party or some other event that was important to them. She also asked them to pretend to read a wordless picture book. She found when these well-read-to children told her about an important event in their lives they used language characteristic of spoken language and when they pretended to read a story they used language more characteristic of written language. Again, we have to assume that the children learned the language of print from others reading to them.

Why should learning the language of print be helpful to learning to read? In Chapter 3, we discussed how children use their knowledge of spoken language to figure out print. Recall Goodman's experiment where children read the same words better in stories than in lists. Recall also Rhodes's findings and Kucer's findings that children read better when provided with reading materials where they can use their knowledge of language to make sense of print. If children use their knowledge of language to figure out print, it follows that when children have acquired the language of print they are in an even better position to figure out print.

A creative experiment by Janet Norris and Roger Bruning (1988) supports this. Norris and Bruning asked kindergarten and first-grade children, some of whom were good beginning readers and some of whom were not, to look at a picture book and then to retell the story to a puppet without the help of the picture book. They found that the children who were better beginning readers told better stories to the puppet than the children who were poorer readers. Presumably the children who were better readers were better readers because they were already familiar with the language of print.

In Kucer's study in Chapter 3 we met a third-grade child who read two stories, one a letter-emphasis, or phonics, story and one a whole language story. As you may recall, for *Once upon a time* she read, "Out open on time." Yet she read phrases like *He called the old woman* with little difficulty. While *He called the old woman* is similar to spoken language, *Once upon a time* is found only in fairy tales (or movie/video versions of fairy tales). The child's difficulty with *Once upon a time* suggests that she had not had many fairy tales read to her.

# Families Who Read to Their Preschool Children—and Families Who Don't

Why, you might ask, do some families read stories to their children and others do not? Probably neither the families who read to their children nor the families who don't are fully aware of the powerful effect reading stories to their children will have on their children's future reading development. Researchers themselves have only recently figured it out. So then, what explains why some families read stories to their children and others don't?

First let's look at families who do read to their children. Parents usually pass on to their children an appreciation of the things they enjoy by involving their children in them as well. Parents who enjoy sports involve their children in sports. Parents who enjoy music involve their children in musical experiences. So it is with parents who enjoy reading. People who have learned to enjoy reading from being read to pass on their enjoyment of reading to their children. Carol Chomsky (1972) interviewed mothers who had read to their children and noticed that the mothers frequently mentioned books from their own childhood that they enjoyed reading to their children.

I asked several women who had read to their young children why they had read to them. Not one of them mentioned teaching their children to read. Rather they all said they read to their children because they enjoyed reading or because they enjoyed reading to their children and their children enjoyed it. One said she wanted her child to appreciate reading. Another said with a chuckle, "Besides, some of the stories are really fun." Still another, a visiting grandmother, said she read to her granddaughter because her granddaughter demanded it. (Mom or Dad had obviously gotten the child "hooked" on the pleasure of reading.)

Try it yourself. Ask parents who read stories to their children why they do it. See if you find similar answers.

In his observations of parent-child interactions in their homes, Wells (1985) notes that when both parents and children enjoy shared book experiences, they are likely to be repeated again and again. Sometimes the children's demands to be read to can reach a point where the parents may have to refuse to read any more stories in order to get their work done.

In sharing their enjoyment of reading with their children, parents who enjoy reading do more than entertain their children: they teach their children that reading is meaningful and they also teach them to understand the language of print. This in turn helps their children learn to read when reading instruction begins in school.

Now let's look at parents who do not read, or seldom read, stories to their children. Some parents who can read seldom read to their children. In Heath's study described in the first section of this chapter, the parents who did not read stories to their children could read. In another study in the United States, Bill Teale (1986) found that of the twenty-four children, ages two and a half to three and a half, from low-income families he studied, all had parents who used reading and writing in their everyday routines such as shopping, paying bills, and reading the TV guide, but only three had parents who read stories to them during the study. (Not coincidentally, the three children in Teale's study who had stories read to them during the study also had mothers who enjoyed reading themselves.) Alonzo Anderson and Shelley Stokes (1984) conducted a similar study with similar findings.

Why do some parents who can read not read, or seldom read, to their children? Wells found that the parents in the Bristol study who did not enjoy reading were unlikely to spend time reading to their children. When they did read to their children, it was viewed more as a chore than a pleasure. Perhaps these parents did not have stories read to them and thus did not have the opportunity to learn the pleasures of print when they were children.

Other researchers have identified another reason why some parents who can read do not read, or seldom read, to their children: they do not have access to age-appropriate books. Courtney Smith, Rebecca Constantino, and Stephen Krashen (1997) looked at homes in one area in California. They found children living in two economically depressed communities had an average of .04 and 2.67 age-appropriate books in the home; those living in a high-income community averaged 199.2 age-appropriate books in the home. They also found the public libraries serving the economically depressed communities had half as many books as those serving the high-income community. Moreover, the school libraries serving the economically depressed communities had one-third to one-fourth as many books as those serving the high-income community.

## Implications for Effective Instruction

The consequence of children never or seldom having stories read to them at home is that they are unlikely to learn at home that reading is meaningful. They are also unlikely to learn the language of print at home. More important, instruction in school, which begins by assuming that children understand that reading is meaningful, is actually meaningless to children who have seldom or never had stories read to them.

It is difficult to overstate the importance of the findings of this line of research. The seemingly benign activity of reading to children is a powerful precursor of literacy. It might be called the first step into literacy. The International Reading Association has summed up the findings of this line of research in one simple motto: Children who read have been read to.

Clearly, we cannot assume that all children who come to school understand the purpose of reading, much less the purpose of a reading lesson. The primary literacy education task of preschool and early school years is not teaching children letter-sound correspondences but reading to them. Reading to children in school should be a daily activity, as important a part of a child's class schedule as math and lunch. If a child is experiencing difficulty in learning to read, we should not ask if he or she knows the sounds of letters but if he or she has been read to extensively.

If a child is experiencing difficulty in learning to read, we should not ask if he or she knows the sounds of letters but if he or she has been read to extensively.

## Helping Children Acquire the Language of Print

It is not just reading to children per se but their comprehension of what they hear that helps them acquire the language of print. In Heath's study (described in the first section of this chapter), in the community where the children were expected to sit still and listen to stories, Heath describes a child who tried to interrupt her parent who was reading to her. The child wanted to talk with her parent about the story. When she was unsuccessful in engaging her parent in a conversation about the story, she climbed down from the couch where they were sitting and ran into the next room saying, "No, no." The child had tried to make sense of what she was hearing by trying to discuss the story with her parent. Failing that, she, quite naturally, escaped an incomprehensible situation by leaving.

Language—in this case, the language of print—is not acquired by listening alone but by making sense of what is heard. In the case of reading to a young child, the experienced reader must make what he or she is saying comprehensible to the child.

How do some parents get young children with limited spoken language to voluntarily listen to and enjoy stories? Bess Altwerger, Judith Diehl-Faxon, and Karen Dockstader-Anderson (1985) studied mothers reading to their children, ages two to two and a half years old. They found that at first the mothers they studied did not read the stories literally to their children.

Rather, they adapted, extended, clarified, and disregarded the language printed in the books, as necessary, to make the story comprehensible to their children. Instead of using the actual language printed in the books, they used language they thought their children would understand based on their children's experiences. Then, as the mothers "read" more and more stories to their children and they judged their children were better able to understand the stories, their readings moved closer and closer to the actual print. Eventually they read literally from the books.

How can children who have rarely had stories read to them at home learn that reading is meaningful and learn to understand the language of print? In the preschool years, one approach is to increase parental access to age-appropriate books for their children and encourage or help parents to read to their preschool children through programs such as Even Start. Another approach is to make the preschool programs such as Head Start that read to children on a daily basis available to all children, but especially to children who might not otherwise have the opportunity to hear stories read to them daily.

Once children are in elementary school we can provide all children the opportunity to discover the pleasures of print by reading to children in school. By ensuring that all children have extensive meaningful experiences hearing stories read to them, schools can help all children learn to understand the language of print as they discover that reading is meaningful. If children who have not been read to in their preschool years learn to enjoy reading in their school years, it is quite probable that when they later become parents they will share their enjoyment of reading with their own children. This in turn will help their children learn that print is meaningful and acquire the language of print.

Dina Feitelson, Bracha Kita, and Zahava Goldstein (1986), who we first met in Chapter 3, carried out an experiment that demonstrated the effect of reading—or not reading—to children in school. They persuaded two teachers working with first-grade children in a school where children tended to do poorly academically to read from series stories to their students the last twenty minutes of the school day. After the experiment began, one teacher stopped reading to her students because she thought it took too much time away from reading instruction. However, the other teacher continued reading to her students the full six months of the experiment. Feitelson and her colleagues found as the experiment was in progress that half the children in the class that was read to spontaneously bought or borrowed copies of the series books and read them during their breaks and free time at school. At the end of the six months Feitelson and her colleagues gave a reading test to the children in the class that had had stories read to them. They gave the same test to the children in the other classes that had not had stories read to them. They found that the children in the class that had had stories read to them daily read better. Rather than taking time away from reading lessons, reading to children was the reading lesson that counted.

In another study, Warwick Elley (1989) asked several second-grade teachers to read one story three times within a week to their students. Even though the teachers did not explain the vocabulary in the stories to their students, Elley found that the children had a 15 percent gain in the vocabulary used in the story.

In still another study, Elley (1991) asked several third-grade teachers to read the same story to their students three times within a week. However, in this study, he asked half of the teachers in the study to explain unfamiliar vocabulary to their students as they encountered it during the reading. Elley again found a 15 percent gain in vocabulary used in the story when the teachers did not explain the vocabulary. However, he also found a hefty 40 percent gain in the vocabulary used in the story when the teachers did explain the vocabulary during the reading.

However, Wells (1986) is convinced that for children who have seldom been read to in their preschool years, "listening to a story read to the whole class is no solution, for they have not yet learned to attend appropriately to written language under such impersonal conditions. For them what is required is one-to-one interaction with an adult centered on a story" (p. 159). From my experience as a primary-grade teacher working with children who had had limited experience in having someone read to them, I concur with Wells. Some schools have programs where volunteers or cross-age tutors visit on a regular basis to engage in one-on-one reading sessions with young children. Others include parents as helpers and send books home for parents to read to their children.

## *Providing Children with Effective Reading Materials*

As children have increased experience with reading—through being read to and through being helped to read—they begin to read stories with familiar language on familiar topics with little or no assistance from more experienced readers. As with any skill, the more they engage in it, the more expert they become. Richard Anderson, Paul Wilson, and Linda Fielding (1988) asked children how much they read at school and at home. Then they compared the amount of time the children spent reading out of school with the children's reading proficiencies. Not surprisingly, they found that the children who read more were better readers. The NAEP study asked similar questions about time spent reading and had similar findings (Mullis, Campbell, and Farstrup 1993).

Why do some children read more than others? Once again, we see a difference in children's access to literacy that affects their reading proficiency. While the intent of public and school library systems is to give equal access to books to everyone regardless of income, there is a growing body of research showing that children in poor communities have less access to age-appropriate books not only at home but also in public and school libraries. Similarly, there is a growing body of research showing that access to age-appropriate books is a powerful predictor of reading achievement.

> Access to age-appropriate books is a powerful predictor of reading achievement.

Jonathan Kozol (1991) found that a public school in New York serving less affluent students had 700 books in the school library for a student body of 1,300 while a neighboring school serving more affluent students had 8,000 books for 825 students. Jeff McQuillan, Noma LeMoine, Eilley Brandlin, and Bonnie O'Brien (1997) sent questionnaires to elementary school libraries in high-achieving and low-achieving schools within the same large school district in California. They found that libraries in the high-achieving schools had larger collections of books and better access policies than libraries in lower-achieving schools.

Stephen Krashen (1995) compared each state's 1992 fourth-grade NAEP scores with the quality of their school libraries, and other factors such as per pupil spending on education. He found a significant positive correlation between the quality of each state's school libraries and its 1992 fourth-grade NAEP reading score, regardless of how much money was spent per pupil. The relationship between access to books and academic achievement continues in high school: McQuillan (1996) found a strong positive correlation between the quality of school and public libraries and average S.A.T. scores. In the IEA study of over 200,000 students in 32 countries described in

Chapter 4, Warwick Elley (1992) found a significant correlation between the quality of school libraries and reading proficiencies in each country, especially in poorer countries.

However, as I point out in Chapter 4, correlation does not establish causation. One way to see if there is a causal relationship between access to books and literacy achievement would be to see what would happen if students who have less access to books are provided more access to books. Warwick Elley and Francis Mangubhai did just that (Elley 1991; Elley and Mangubhai 1983). They provided children learning English as a subsequent language who otherwise had limited access to age-appropriate books in English with large quantities of books. They found significant growth in their reading proficiencies. One of the things the teachers in Anderson, Wilson, and Fieldings's study, described earlier in this chapter, did to promote reading was to assure their students had access to interesting books at a suitable level of difficulty.

> Researchers provided children who had limited access to age-appropriate books with large quantities of books and found significant growth in their reading proficiencies.

In an economically depressed neighborhood, the National Reading Research Center provided first-grade children attending low-literacy-achieving schools with classroom libraries and encouraged the children to take books home to their parents (Gambrell 1996). At the end of the ten-week study, the children who participated in the study were more motivated to read and spent more time reading independently and with family members than children in the control classes. Furthermore, the effects appeared to be long lasting. Six months after the study the children still spent more time reading than their counterparts who had not participated in the study and, perhaps most important, perceived themselves as more competent readers than children who had not participated in the study.

In their study of elementary school libraries cited above, McQuillan, LeMoine, Brandlin, and O'Brien write poignantly about the findings of their study:

Children from less wealthy homes must . . . rely on the school library to supply them with materials to read. It is therefore ironic and tragic that children in the schools precisely where library access is most critical have much more restricted access to books than those who already have, on average, available sources of print. (p. 25)

When we remember that more than 20 percent of children in the United States live in poverty (Berliner and Biddle 1995, p. 217), this observation becomes a compelling argument for our responsibility to provide all children with access to age-appropriate books.

This line of research suggests that if some groups of fourth-grade children are scoring lower on reading tests relative to other groups of children, we should not ask if they have had explicit, systematic, extensive instruction in phonics, but if they and their families have access to age-appropriate books. It suggests that when California's 1995 Reading Task Force called for 1,500 books per classroom, they were pointing to a powerful way to improve reading instruction. It suggests that it would be more cost-effective for states and school districts to spend their money, not on sets of "core reading program instructional materials . . . [that] include systematic, explicit [traditional] phonics," as California's AB 3482 mandates and training teachers and their supervising administrators on traditional phonics instruction, but on stocking classrooms with engaging, age-appropriate books on a wide variety of topics.

# 8

# Beyond Traditional Phonics

THIS BOOK HAS PRESENTED A RESEARCH-BASED VIEW OF HOW children learn to read that is fundamentally different from our traditional assumptions. It has presented research evidence that

- children learn to read by being read to and by reading;
- early readers read better in the context of familiar language than outside of such context;
- as children learn to recognize more and more print words in the context of familiar language they use their knowledge of words they already recognize to pronounce words they don't recognize;
- the more children read, the more proficient readers they become.

Altogether the research says that, instructionally, the three most important things we can do to help children learn to read are the following:

- read to them, adjusting our reading to their comprehension needs;
- help them get started in their own reading via instructional techniques such as shared reading with predictable stories;
- provide them with access to engaging, age-appropriate books.

The research also says that if children are having trouble reading stories with familiar language on topics familiar to them, we need to ask the following questions:

- Have they been read to extensively one-on-one by more experienced readers and have they had opportunities to discuss the stories?

- Have they been helped to read extensively through instructional strategies such as shared reading with predictable stories?
- Have they had extensive access to age-appropriate books?

When the answer to any of these questions is "no," we need to provide the experiences. Finally, this book has presented research evidence that, contrary to our deeply held cultural beliefs, children have difficulty analyzing spoken words into phonemes when there is more than one phoneme in an onset or a rime. This research says that instruction in letter-phoneme correspondences is difficult, at best, for children and not the most effective way to help children become literate.

In this final chapter, I would like to offer some thoughts on (1) the role of phonics in spelling instruction and (2) how we might teach children phonics in a way that is compatible with what we now know about how children learn letter-sound correspondences.

## *Reconceptualizing Spelling "Rules"*

Does phonics instruction help children spell? In Chapter 2, I elaborated on the inconsistencies of our spelling system. One of the ways I like to demonstrate these inconsistencies when I talk to groups of people is to ask them to say all the words they can think of that rhyme with the word *blue*. As they call off the words, I write the words on an overhead projector with the projector light off. When they finish, I turn the projector light on and we see the many ways that the /oo/ sound can be spelled, e.g., *ue* in *blue, glue,* and *sue; ew* in *threw, stew,* and *new; o* in *do, to,* and *two; oo* in *too, zoo,* and *moo; ough* in *through; oe* in *shoe; u* in *menu;* and *ous* in *rendezvous.*

Some people suggest we should standardize our spelling system, but whose dialect should it reflect? Should we create a spelling system to be consistent with a Boston accent? A Texan accent? A New York accent? A midwestern accent? And what would we do with words like *knowledge* and *breakfast* where their spellings reflect their meanings, not their pronunciations? Should we abandon the clues to meaning in order to rewrite them phonetically?

Efforts to find (or create) reliable spelling-sound generalizations implicitly assume that spelling is rule governed in the same way that natural phenomena, such as gravity or electricity, are rule governed. This assumption is reflected in phrases such as *phonics rules*, *spelling principles*, and *the alphabetic principle*.

> Modern spelling is better understood, not as an inherently principled system but as a set of arbitrary, socially agreed on conventions specific to each word.

Modern spelling is better understood, not as an inherently principled system but as a set of arbitrary, socially agreed on conventions specific to each word. "American spelling" was intentionally created by Americans in the nineteenth century to distinguish American literature from British literature (Goodman 1993, p. 42). If one looks at the history of writing from ancient Egypt to modern times, standardized spelling is a recent social phenomena. In the seventeenth century *cat, catte, kat, katt,* and *katte* were all used to represent *cat.* Shakespeare, one of the great English writers of all time, signed his name with two different spellings on the same document (Cummings 1988, p. 21; cited in Goodman 1993, p. 41). Then, gradually, just as modern societies standardized measurements of length, volume, temperature, electricity, clothing, wood, and paper, they standardized spelling. That is, the English-speaking world standardized the spelling of the word *cat* as *cat,* not as *catt, catte, kat, katt,* or *katte.* Today's generation of literate adults were taught by the previous generation of literate adults (who in turn were taught by yet another generation of literate adults) that there is only one acceptable spelling of *cat.* While it is now a socially agreed on convention in Western cultures that each person spells his or her name the same way every time, we still allow variation among people with the same name; the spell check on my word processing program recognizes *Katharine, Katherine, Kathryn,* and *Catherine.* We even allow parents to be "creative" in the spelling of their children's names, for example, *Robyn* for *Robin.* Businesses frequently use creative spelling in their names and slogans (e.g., 25 YEARS OF LUV) but in their creativeness they are consistent (e.g., *love* is always spelled *luv* in 25 YEARS OF LUV).

Why do we teach children to spell *cat* as *cat* rather than, for instance, *kat* or *catt* or *catte*? If *kaleidoscope, kangaroo, Karen, katydid, kayak, kilogram,* and many other words with a /k/ sound are spelled with a *k*, why can't *cat* be spelled with a *k*? If *mat* can be spelled *matt* or *matte* (*Webster's New Collegiate Dictionary* 1981), why can't *cat* be spelled *catt* or *catte*? The truth is, it could have been. Our forefathers just happened to agree that it would be spelled *cat*, and they standardized the spelling of *cat*. They could have just as well agreed that it would be *kat* or *catt* or *catte*, but they didn't.

Whether *blue* is written *bloe* (as in *shoe*), or *blo* (as in *to*), or *bloo* (as in *too*), or *blue* is an arbitrary, socially agreed on convention. This is not to say that a given word can be written any old way. The word *blue* cannot be written *lbue*. There are multiple possible ways to represent spoken sounds in English. Which way is used in a particular print word is an arbitrary, social convention.

It is not too hard to see how, as the printing press emerged in the industrial age, standardizing spelling helped typesetters. Something that we may be less aware of is how standardized spelling also helps us as readers. Read the following sentence written with phonetically possible but nonstandard spelling.

Shee livz n shikago with a blak kat.

Could you read it? Although *shee, livz, n, shikago, blak,* and *kat* are phonetically possible renditions of *she, lives, in, Chicago, black,* and *cat,* they are not conventional renditions. Now read the following sentence:

He lives in Chicago with a white dog.

Did you notice how much easier it was to read *He lives in Chicago with a white dog* than *Shee livz n shikago with a blak kat*? Conventional spelling is familiar spelling. Read *Shee livz n shikago with a blak kat* several times and see how much easier it gets as it becomes more familiar to you. Conventional spelling is easier to read than unconventional spelling just as typed messages are easier to read than hand-written messages. We readers have to work harder to make sense out of messages written with unconventional spelling or messages written by hand. If the spelling or handwriting are too different from conventional norms, it can be irritating to try to figure it out. Standardized spelling facilitates reading.

Another benefit of standardized spelling is that it can be read across dialects within a larger language community. In the U.S., Bostonians can read (and write for) the *Los Angeles Times* just as easily as they read (and write for) the *New York Times*. Texans can read (and write for) the *Chicago Tribune* just as easily as they read the CNN credits broadcast from Atlanta, Georgia. Despite our various regional dialects, we all read and write the same conventionalized script.

When children are struggling to spell conventionally during the editing phase of their writing, we mislead them when we ask them to "sound out" words. In my dialect, a child struggling to spell *shoe* by "sounding it out" can just as legitimately spell *shoe* as *sho* (as in *to*), *shew* (as in *new*), *shue* (as in *blue*) or *shoe*. A child who writes *for a speshel dance techer* will not benefit from instructions to "sound out" the spelling of *special* and *teacher*. She already has: *speshel* and *techer* are phonetically possible renditions of *special* and *teacher*. They just don't happen to be conventional.

Rather than asking children to sound out words when we are trying to foster conventional spelling, we might better guide them to use their visual memory. We might ask questions such as "Does that look right?" or "Can you remember what it looks like?" or "Can you remember seeing that word somewhere?" Alternately, we might encourage them to write the word in question several ways and see which one looks right.

## *Whole-to-Parts Phonics Instruction*

How can we use the research discoveries reported in this book about how children learn letter-sound correspondences so that we can teach children letter-sound correspondences in a way that supports and enhances their natural learning processes? First, let us quickly review the research findings. In Chapter 2, we examined research evidence that children who have not yet learned to read have difficulty analyzing spoken words into phonemes. We also looked at research findings on the complexity of our letter-sound system. Then, in Chapter 5, we reviewed exciting new research evidence that children spontaneously figure out how to pronounce unfamiliar print words by recognizing parts in the unfamiliar words that are similar to parts in words they already recognize. We also reviewed evidence that onsets and rimes are the psychological units of the English syllable and that the parts of words children use to make analogies between familiar and unfamiliar words in English are letters representing onsets and rimes, not phonemes. I suggested that this process of using familiar words to pronounce unfamiliar words accounts for why children without traditional phonics instruction who are being helped to read stories with language that is familiar to them actually acquire the letter-sound system better than children whose programs emphasize letter-phoneme correspondences.

At first I reasoned, why teach children to do something they already do just because we adults have finally figured it out (Moustafa 1993)? Then I remembered, when we learned that children use their knowledge of language to read, we created predictable stories with familiar language and that helped children learn to read. I also remembered, when we learned that children use their knowledge of the world to help them make sense of print, we provided them with knowledge on unfamiliar topics before they read on the unfamiliar topics and that helped children make sense of print. What if we were to teach letter-sound correspondences by showing children the parts of familiar words that represent the psychological parts of speech?

Here I would like to propose teaching letter-sound correspondences in a systematic way that is compatible with what we now know about how children acquire letter-sound correspondences. In Chapter 5, I reviewed research that shows the more print words children recognize the better position they are in to make analogies between familiar and unfamiliar print words to pronounce unfamiliar print words. I then suggested that shared reading with predictable stories is a powerful way of helping children acquire a lot of print words so that they can begin to make analogies. The print words that become familiar to children through shared reading are an ideal place to begin systematic instruction in letter-sound correspondences.

> As more and more words are put on the wall, the teacher and children can collaboratively group together words with similar letters or letter strings.

After a teacher has read a predictable story *to* and *with* children and the children have learned to read the story *by themselves*, the teacher can ask the children to choose their favorite words in the story. The teacher teaching children to read in English can then write each word on a separate piece of paper, highlight letters representing an onset (e.g., *sm-*) or a rime (e.g., *-iles*) and tell the children "These letters say /sm/" or "These letters say /ilz/" and put the words on the classroom wall.[1] As more and more words are put on the wall, the teacher and children can collaboratively group together words with similar letters or letter strings. That is, if *go*, *girl*, and *get* are words that children have chosen from the stories they have learned to read and the teacher has highlighted the *g* in each of these words, these words would be grouped together. This grouping helps children make letter-sound generalities based on words they have learned to recognize in context. When multiple pronunciations of given letters or letter strings come up, the teacher can use different colors to highlight the various pronunciations (e.g., highlight the *g-* in *girl* and *go* in one color and the *g-* in *giant* and *George* in another color). As more and more stories are read *to*, *with*, and *by* children, they learn more and more parts of words as well as multiple ways to pronounce given letters and letter strings. This word wall is similar to Cunningham's (1995) word wall except the words on the wall are constantly being regrouped by teachers and children together as more and more words go up on the wall and, as described below, there is always a logo next to each word.

A teacher teaching children to read in Spanish, a language that is not an onset-rime language, can use a similar strategy to teach letter-sound correspondences in Spanish. Again, after a predictable story is read *to*, *with*, and *by* children, the teacher can ask the children for their favorite words in the story. Then, rather than highlighting letters that represent onsets or rimes, the teacher can highlight letters representing the psychologically salient unit in Spanish, syllables, (e.g., *ca-* or *-sa* in *casa*) and tell the children "These letters say /ka/" or "These letters say /sa/."

Because early readers have difficulty identifying print words out of con-

> Whole-to-parts phonics instruction teaches the parts of the words after a story has been read *to*, *with*, and *by* children.

---

[1]Thanks to Patricia Cunningham (1995) and Janiel Wagstaff (1996) for their pioneering work with word walls and instruction in onset-rime analogy. While the instructional strategy described here differs from Cunningham's and Wagstaff's, it was inspired by them.

text, as more and more words go up on the wall, there is a danger of print words getting lost in a sea of words. A little logo next to each word representing the story the word came from will help the children remember the story where they encountered each word. One easy way to do this is to fold an 8½-by-11-inch piece of paper lengthwise to create two 4¼-by-11-inch sections, unfold the paper, and tape a picture representing a predictable story on the left-hand side of each section of the paper. This "master" sheet can then be photocopied several times, and the photocopies can be cut lengthwise into two 4¼-by-11-inch pieces. This creates a set of blank pieces of paper with a logo from a predictable story on the left-hand side. These blank pieces of paper are then ready for the teacher to write words on them as the children choose words from the stories they have learned to read.

A flexible system of displaying the words facilitates collaborative re-

| Traditional | Whole-to-Parts |
|---|---|
| systematic, explicit, extensive | systematic, explicit, extensive |
| based on assumptions dating back to Socrates | based on recent discoveries in linguistics and psychology |
| goes from parts to whole (from letters to words) | goes from whole to parts (from whole text, to words, to word parts) |
| instruction occurs before reading | instruction occurs after reading (e.g., after a predictable story is read to, with, and by children) |
| teaches letter-phoneme correspondences | teaches letter-psychological parts of speech correspondences (in English, letter-onset and letter-rime correspondences; in Spanish, letter-syllable correspondences) |
| teaches inconsistent rules | teaches multiple possibilities |
| abstract, difficult to remember | contextualized, memorable |
| logical, makes sense to literate adults | psychological, makes sense to children learning to read |

*Figure 8.1 Phonics Instruction*

grouping of the words as more and more of them go up on the wall. One strategy is to secure a plastic shower curtain liner to the classroom wall. Then as the children choose the words and the teacher highlights parts of the words, the teacher can attach the words to the plastic liner with transparent tape placed horizontally on the upper edge of the paper. The tape attaches and reattaches to the plastic quickly and easily allowing for easy regrouping.

I call this way of teaching letter-sound correspondences *whole-to-parts phonics instruction*. In many ways, whole-to-parts phonics instruction looks like traditional phonics instruction. However, as Figure 8.1 shows, it is radically different. Whole-to-parts phonics instruction differs from traditional phonics instruction in that (1) it teaches the parts of the words after a story has been read *to*, *with*, and *by* children rather than before the story is read by children, and (2) it teaches the psychological units of the syllable (in English, letter-onset and letter-rime correspondences; in Spanish, syllables) rather than letter-phoneme correspondences. Yet, like traditional phonics instruction, it is explicit, systematic, and extensive. More important, it is psycholinguistically appropriate. It is an instructional method that may finally lay to rest the phonics argument that has plagued the history of reading instruction for centuries.

# Epilogue

# Beyond the Groan Zone

THE RESEARCH DISCOVERIES OF THE LAST FORTY YEARS HAVE provided us with new, counterintuitive understandings of how children learn to read. Research has consistently shown that early readers read better in the context of familiar language than outside of such context (Nicholson 1991; Stanovich 1991). Research has also consistently shown that children's experiences with age-appropriate books vary and that access to and enjoyable experiences with books affect reading proficiency (Elley 1991, 1992, 1994; Heath 1982, 1983; Krashen 1995; Wells 1985).

In this book, I have shown that shared reading with predictable stories is a powerful teaching strategy that enables early readers to become proficient readers. I have shown how shared reading with predictable stories can enable children to acquire the letter-sound system faster and more effectively than traditional phonics instruction. Finally, I proposed whole-to-parts phonics instruction as a research-grounded alternative to traditional phonics instruction.

Unfortunately, the public in general and our policy makers, political leaders, and the press, in particular, are not yet informed of these counterintuitive research discoveries. As political events of the past few years have shown, it is not enough for educators to understand these important discoveries and their instructional implications. Effective reading instruction requires both knowledgeable teachers and appropriate instructional materials.

Books—predictable books for early readers and engaging age-appropriate books for all readers—are the infrastructure that support effective reading instruction. Books are as important to literacy education as food is to a school cafeteria and as highways are to industry. In a democracy such as ours, providing an appropriate infrastructure to support effective reading instruction requires that the public, press, and policy makers understand the research discoveries that are so different from our traditional assumptions. For it is only when the public, press, and policy makers understand what has been discovered about how children learn to read and the implications of these discoveries for instruction that their well-intended actions will be translated into appropriate support for knowledgeable educators.

> Providing an appropriate infrastructure to support effective reading instruction requires that the public, press, and policy makers understand the research discoveries that are so different from our traditional assumptions.

Currently we are in a groan zone. Concerned citizens who are not yet aware of the amazing research discoveries outlined in this book are promoting policies that make reading instruction less effective rather than more effective.

How can we move beyond this groan zone into more effective reading education? In the short run, we can ask our policy makers to look beyond the recommendations of advisors and reach out and consult with the leadership of mainstream professional organizations concerned with literacy education such as the International Reading Association and the National Council of Teachers of English.

In the long run, we can help the public in general and policy makers in particular understand these counterintuitive discoveries about how children learn to read. We can begin by offering college courses on reading and developmental literacy in liberal arts programs. Most of our future political leaders, policy makers, and members of the media will major in liberal arts. We can also include information about literacy development in high school parenting classes.

We will move beyond the groan zone into a new age of effective reading instruction in our public schools, once the seminal discoveries described in this book become common knowledge to the public and our leadership. Won't you tell a friend?

# References

Adams, M. J. 1990. *Beginning to Read: Thinking and Learning About Print.* Cambridge, MA: MIT Press.

Allington, R. L. 1983. "The Reading Instruction Provided Readers of Different Reading Abilities." *Elementary School Journal* 83: 95–107.

Altwerger, B., J. Diehl-Faxon, and K. Dockstader-Anderson. 1985. "Read-Aloud Events as Meaning Construction." *Language Arts* 62: 476–484.

Anderson, A., and S. Stokes. 1984. "Social and Institutional Influences on the Development and Practice of Literacy." In *Awakening to Literacy.* Eds. H. Goelman, A. A. Oberg, and F. Smith. Portsmouth, NH: Heinemann.

Anderson, R. C., I. A. G. Wilkinson, and J. M. Mason. 1991. "A Microanalysis of the Small-Group, Guided Reading Lesson: Effects of an Emphasis on Global Story Meaning." *Reading Research Quarterly* XXVI: 417–441.

Anderson, R. C., P. T. Wilson, and L. G. Fielding. 1988. "Growth in Reading and How Children Spend Their Time Outside of School." *Reading Research Quarterly* XXIII: 285–303.

Arnold, D. J., and P. H. Brooks. 1976. "Influence of Contextual Organizing Material on Children's Listening Comprehension." *Journal of Educational Psychology* 68: 711–716.

Associated Press. 1995. "State Tops in Ranking of Worst." *San Francisco Chronicle,* July 15, A15, A17.

Bailey, M. H. 1967. "The Utility of Phonic Generalizations in Grades One Through Six." *The Reading Teacher* 20: 413–418.

Balmuth, M. 1982. *The Roots of Phonics.* New York: Teachers College Press.

Bartlett, F. C. 1932. *Remembering: A Study in Experimental and Social Psychology.* New York: Cambridge University Press.

Bay, W. 1996. Feature news story on reading instruction. *Good Morning America.* American Broadcasting Company, 21 November.

Beck, I. L., R. C. Omanson, and M. G. McKeown. 1982. "An Instructional Redesign of Reading Lessons: Effects on Comprehension." *Reading Research Quarterly* IV: 462–481.

Berdiansky, B., B. Cronnell, and J. Koehler. 1969. *Spelling-Sound Relations and Primary Form-Class Descriptions for Speech Comprehension Vocabularies of 6–9 Year Olds*. Technical Report No. 15. Los Alamitos, CA: Southwest Regional Laboratory for Educational Research and Development.

Berliner, D. C., and B. J. Biddle. 1995. *The Manufactured Crisis*. New York: Addison-Wesley.

Binkley, M., and T. Williams. 1996. *Reading Literacy in the United States: Findings from the IEA Reading Literacy Study*. Washington, D.C.: U.S. Department of Education, Office of Educational Research and Improvement.

Bond, G. L., and R. Dykstra. 1967. "The Cooperative Research Program in First-Grade Reading Instruction." *Reading Research Quarterly* II: 5–142.

Bransford, J. D., and M. K. Johnson. 1972. "Contextual Prerequisites for Understanding: Some Investigations of Comprehension and Recall." *Journal of Verbal Learning and Verbal Behavior* 11: 711–726.

Brown, A. L., S. S. Smiley, J. D. Day, M. A. Townsend, and S. C. Lawton. 1977. "Intrusion of the Thematic Idea in Children's Comprehension and Retention of Stories." *Child Development* 48: 1454–1466.

Bruce, D. J. 1964. "The Analysis of Word Sounds." *British Journal of Educational Psychology* 34: 158–170.

Burmeister, L. E. 1968. "Usefulness of Phonic Generalizations." *The Reading Teacher* 21: 349–356.

Calfee, R. 1977. "Assessment of Individual Reading Skills: Basic Research and Practical Applications." In *Toward a Psychology of Reading*. Eds. A. S. Reber and D. L. Scarborough. New York: Lawrence Erlbaum.

California Department of Education. 1987. *English-Language Arts Framework*. Sacramento: California Department of Education.

———. 1988. *Instructional Materials and Framework Adoption: Policies and Procedures*. Sacramento: California Department of Education.

———. 1987/1994. *English-Language Arts Framework*. Sacramento: California Department of Education.

———. 1995. *Every Child a Reader*. Sacramento: California Department of Education.

California State Board of Education. 1996. *The California Reading Initiative* [Prepublication of the California State Board's Statement, September 13, 1996]. Sacramento: California Department of Education.

Cattell, J. M. 1886. "The Time Taken Up by Cerebral Operations." *Mind* 11: 220–242.

———. 1947. "The Inertia of the Eye and Brain." In *James McKeen Cattell: Man of Science*. Ed. A. T. Poffenberger. New York: Science Press.

Chall, J. S. 1967. *Learning to Read: The Great Debate*. New York: McGraw Hill.

Chen, E., and R. L. Colvin. 1996. "Dole Sees Problems in Schools and Blames Liberals." *Los Angeles Times*, 18 July.

Chiesi, H. L., G. J. Spilich, and J. F. Voss. 1979. "Acquisition of Domain-Related Information in Relation to High and Low Domain Knowledge." *Journal of Verbal Learning and Verbal Behavior* 18: 257–273.

Chomsky, C. 1972. "Stages in Language Development and Reading Exposure." *Harvard Educational Review* 42: 1–33.

Clymer, T. 1963. "The Utility of Phonic Generalizations in the Primary Grades." *The Reading Teacher* 16: 252–258.

Collier, V. P. 1989. "How Long? A Synthesis of Research on Academic Achievement in a Second Language." *TESOL Quarterly* 23 (3): 509–531.

Colvin, R. L. 1995a. "State Report Urges Return to Basics in Teaching Reading." *Los Angeles Times*, 13 September, Orange County Edition.

————. 1995b. "Her Best Subject." *Los Angeles Times*, 19 November, Orange County Edition.

Crafton, L. 1983. "Learning from Reading: What Happens When Students Generate Their Own Background Information." *Journal of Reading* 586–592.

Cummings, D. W. 1988. *American English Spelling: An Informal Description*. Baltimore, MD: The Johns Hopkins University Press.

Cunningham, P. M. 1995. *Phonics They Use*. New York: HarperCollins.

Dolch, E. W. 1945. *A Manual for Remedial Reading*. Champaign, IL: Garrard.

Durkin, D. 1961. "Children Who Read Before Grade One." *The Reading Teacher* 14: 163–166.

————. 1987. "Influences on Basal Reader Programs." *Elementary School Journal* 87: 331–341.

Ehri, L. C., and L. S. Wilce. 1980. "The Influence of Orthography on Readers' Conceptualization of the Phonemic Structure of Words." *Applied Psycholinguistics* 1: 371–385.

————. 1985. "Movement into Reading: Is the First Stage of Printed Word Learning Visual or Phonetic?" *Reading Research Quarterly* XX: 163–179.

Elley, W. B. 1989. "Vocabulary Acquisition from Listening to Stories." *Reading Research Quarterly* XXIV: 174–187.

————. 1991. "Acquiring Literacy in a Second Language: The Effect of Book-Based Programs." *Language Learning* 41 (3): 375–411.

————. 1992. *How in the World Do Students Read? The IEA Study of Reading Literacy*. The Hague, Netherlands: International Associations for the Evaluation of Educational Achievement.

————. 1994. *The IEA Study of Reading Literacy: Achievement and Instruction in Thirty-Two School Systems*. Oxford: Pergamon.

Elley, W. B., and F. Mangubhai. 1983. "The Impact of Reading on Second Language Learning." *Reading Research Quarterly* XIX: 53–67.

Emans, R. 1967. "The Usefulness of Phonic Generalizations Above the Primary Grades." *The Reading Teacher* 20: 419–425.

Erdmann, B., and R. Dodge. 1898. "Psychologische Untersuchungen uber das Lesen, auf Experimenteller Grundlage." In *The Psychology and Pedagogy of Reading*. Ed. E. B. Huey. Cambridge, MA: MIT Press.

Feitelson, D., B. Kita, and Z. Goldstein. 1986. "Effects of Listening to Series Stories on First Graders' Comprehension and Use of Language." *Research in the Teaching of English* 20: 339–356.

Feitelson, D., and Z. Goldstein. 1986. "Patterns of Book Ownership and Reading to Young Children in Israeli School-Oriented and Nonschool-Oriented Families." *The Reading Teacher* 39: 924–930.

Flesch, Rudolph. 1955. *Why Johnny Can't Read*. New York: Harper and Row.

———. 1979. "Why Johnny *Still* Can't Read." *Family Circle* 26: 43–44, 46.

Freepon, P. 1991. "Children's Concepts of the Nature and Purpose of Reading in Different Instructional Settings." *Journal of Reading Behavior* 23 (2): 139–163.

Gambrell, L. B. 1996. "Creating Classroom Cultures That Foster Reading Motivation." *The Reading Teacher* 50 (1): 14–25.

Ginsburg, H., and S. Opper. 1979. *Piaget's Theory of Intellectual Development*. Englewood Cliffs, NJ: Prentice-Hall.

Goodman, K. 1965. "A Linguistic Study of Cues and Miscues in Reading." *Elementary English* 42: 639–643.

———. 1993. *Phonics Phacts*. Portsmouth, NH: Heinemann.

Goodman, K. S., and Y. M. Goodman. 1979. "Learning to Read is Natural." In *Theory and Practice of Early Reading*. Vol. 1. Eds. L. Resnick and P. A. Weaver. Hillsdale, NJ: Lawrence Erlbaum.

Goodman, Y. M. 1986. "Children Coming to Know Literacy." In *Emergent Literacy: Writing and Reading*. Eds. W. H. Teale and E. Sulzby. Norwood, NJ: Ablex.

Goswami, U. 1986. "Children's Use of Analogy in Learning to Read: A Developmental Study." *Journal of Experimental Child Psychology* 42: 73–83.

———. 1988. "Orthographic Analogies and Reading Development." *The Quarterly Journal of Experimental Psychology* 40A: 239–268.

Goswami, U., and P. Bryant. 1990. *Phonological Skills and Learning to Read*. Hillsdale, NJ: Lawrence Erlbaum.

Goswami, U., and F. Mead. 1992. "Onset and Rime Awareness and Analogies in Reading." *Reading Research Quarterly* 27: 150–162.

Hanania, J. 1995. "Sinking Scores? Not in the Numbers." *Los Angeles Times*, 28 May.

Harste, J. C., C. L. Burke, and V. A. Woodward. 1982. "Children's Language and World: Initial Encounters with Print." In *Reader Meets Author: Bridging the Gap*. Eds. J. A. Langer and M. T. Smith-Burke. Newark, DE: International Reading Association.

Heath, S. B. 1982. "What No Bedtime Story Means: Narrative Skills at Home and School." *Language in Society* II: 49–76.

———. 1983. *Ways with Words*. New York: Cambridge University Press.

Hiebert, E. H. 1983. "An Examination of Ability Grouping for Reading Instruction." *Reading Research Quarterly* XVIII: 231–255.

Holdaway, D. 1979. *The Foundations of Literacy*. Portsmouth, NH: Heinemann.

Huey, E. B. 1968. *The Psychology and Pedagogy of Reading*. Cambridge, MA: MIT Press.

Jiang, S., and B. Li. 1985. "A Glimpse at Reading Instruction in China." *The Reading Teacher* 38: 762–766.

Kimura, Y., and P. Bryant. 1983. "Reading and Writing in English and Japanese." *British Journal of Developmental Psychology* 1: 143–153.

Knight, H. 1997. "U.S. Immigrant Level at Highest Peak Since '30s." *Los Angeles Times*, 9 April.

Kozol, J. 1991. *Savage Inequalities*. New York: Crown.

Krashen, S. 1995. "School Libraries, Public Libraries, and the NAEP Reading Scores." *School Library Media Quarterly* 23: 235–237.

Kucer, S. B. 1985. "Predictability and Readability: The Same Rose with Different Names?" In *Claremont Reading Conference Forty-Ninth Yearbook*. Ed. M. Douglass. Claremont, CA: Claremont Graduate School.

Kuhn, T. 1970. *The Structure of Scientific Revolutions*. Chicago: University of Chicago.

Lee, D., and R. Van Allen. 1963. *Learning to Read Through Experience*. New York: Appleton-Century-Crofts.

Liberman, I., D. Shankweiler, F. W. Fischer, and B. Carter. 1974. "Explicit Syllable and Phoneme Segmentation in the Young Child." *Journal of Experimental Child Psychology* 18: 201–212.

Lipson, M. Y. 1983. "The Influence of Religious Affiliation on Children's Memory for Text Information." *Reading Research Quarterly* XVIII: 448–457.

MacKay, D. G. 1972. "The Structure of Words and Syllables: Evidence from Errors in Speech." *Cognitive Psychology* 3: 210–227.

Mann, V. A. 1986. "Phonological Awareness: The Role of Reading Experience." *Cognition* 24: 65–92.

Marr, M. B., and K. Gormley. 1982. "Children's Recall of Familiar and Unfamiliar Text." *Reading Research Quarterly* XVIII: 89–104.

*McGuffey's Eclectic Primer*. Rev. ed. 1909. New York: Van Nostrand Reinhold.

McQuillan, J. 1996. "SAT Verbal Scores and the Library: Predicting High School Reading Achievement in the United States." *Indiana Media Journal* 18 (3): 65–70.

McQuillan, J., N. LeMoine, E. Brandlin, and B. O'Brien. 1997. "The (Print-) Rich Get Richer: Library Access in Low- and High-Achieving Elementary Schools." *The California Reader* 30 (2): 23–25.

Moustafa, M. 1990. *An Interactive/Cognitive Model of the Acquisition of a Graphophonemic System by Young Children*. Ph.D. Dissertation, University of Southern California.

———. 1993. "Recoding in Whole Language Reading Instruction." *Language Arts* 70: 483–487.

———. 1995. "Children's Productive Phonological Recoding." *Reading Research Quarterly* 30 (3): 464–476.

Mullis, I., J. Campbell, and A. Farstrup. 1993. *NAEP 1992 Reading Report Card for the Nation and the States*. Washington, D.C.: National Center for Education Statistics.

New Basic Readers. *We Work and Play*. 1956. Chicago, IL: Scott, Foresman.

Nicholson, T. 1991. "Do Children Read Words Better in Context or in Lists? A Classic Study Revisited." *Journal of Educational Psychology* 83: 444–450.

Nicholson, T., C. Lillas, and M. A. Rzoska. 1988. "Have We Been Misled by Miscues?" *The Reading Teacher* 42: 6–10.

Norris, J. A., and R. H. Bruning. 1988. "Cohesion in the Narratives of Good and Poor Readers." *Journal of Speech and Hearing Disorders* 53: 416–424.

Nye, B. A., J. B. Zaharias, B. D. Fulton, M. P. Wallenhorst, C. M. Achilles, and R. Hooper. 1992. *Lasting Benefits Study: A Continuing Analysis of the Effects of Small Class Size in Kindergarten Through Third Grade on Student Achievement Test Scores in Subsequent Grade Levels: Fifth Grade Executive Summary*. ERIC, ED 354992.

Omanson, R. C., I. L. Beck, J. F. Voss, and M. G. McKeown. 1984. "The Effects of Reading Lessons on Comprehension: A Processing Description." *Cognition and Instruction* 1: 45–67.

Pearson, P. D., J. Hansen, and C. Gordon. 1979. "The Effect of Background Knowledge on Young Children's Comprehension of Explicit and Implicit Information." *Journal of Reading Behavior* 11: 201–209.

Pillsbury, W. B. 1897. "A Study in Apperception." *American Journal of Psychology* 8: 315–393.

Purcell-Gates, V. 1988. "Lexical and Syntactic Knowledge of Written Narrative Held by Well-Read-to-Kindergartners and Second Graders." *Research in the Teaching of English* 22: 128–160.

Recht, D. R., and L. Leslie. 1988. "Effect of Prior Knowledge on Good and Poor Readers' Memory of Text." *Journal of Educational Psychology* 80: 16–20.

Reicher, G. M. 1969. "Perceptual Recognition as a Function of Meaningfulness of Stimulus Materials." *Journal of Experimental Psychology* 81: 275–280.

Resnick, D., and L. Resnick. 1977. "The Nature of Literacy: An Historical Exploration." *Harvard Educational Review* 47: 370–385.

Reutzel, D. R., and R. B. Cooter. 1990. "Whole Language: Comparative Effects on First-Grade Reading Achievement." *Journal of Educational Research* 83: 252–257.

Rhodes, L. K. 1979. "Comprehension and Predictability: An Analysis of Beginning Reading Materials." In *New Perspectives on Comprehension*. (Monograph in Language and Reading Studies). Bloomington: Indiana University School of Education.

———. 1981. "I Can Read! Predictable Books as Resources for Reading and Writing Instruction." *The Reading Teacher* 34: 511–518.

Ribowsky, H. 1986. *The Comparative Effects of a Code Emphasis Approach and a Whole Language Approach upon Emergent Literacy of Kindergarten Children*. Ph.D. Dissertation, New York University.

Richek, M. A., and B. K. McTague. 1988. "The 'Curious George' Strategy for Students with Reading Problems." *The Reading Teacher* 42: 220–226.

Risko, V. J., and M. C. Alvarez. 1986. "An Investigation of Poor Readers' Use of a Thematic Strategy to Comprehend Text." *Reading Research Quarterly* XXI: 298–316.

Roberts, T. A. 1988. "Development of Pre-Instruction Versus Previous Experience: Effects on Factual and Inferential Comprehension." *Reading Psychology* 9: 141–157.

Rosner, J. 1974. "Auditory Analysis Training with Prereaders." *The Reading Teacher* 27: 379–384.

Rosow, L. 1988. "Adult Illiterates Offer Unexpected Cues into the Reading Process." *Journal of Reading* 32: 120–124.

Ruddell, R. B. 1965. "The Effect of Oral and Written Patterns of Language Structure on Reading Comprehension." *The Reading Teacher* 18: 270–275.

Rumelhart, D. E. 1985. "Toward an Interactive Model of Reading." In *Theoretical Models and Processes of Reading*. 3d ed. Eds. R. Barr, M. L. Kamil, P. Mosenthal, and P. D. Pearson. Newark, DE: International Reading Association.

Schuberth, R. E., and P. D. Eimas. 1977. "Effects of Context on the Classification of Words and Nonwords." *Journal of Experimental Psychology: Human Perception and Performance* 3: 27–36.

Smith, C., R. Constantino, and S. Krashen. 1997. "Differences in Print Environment for Children in Beverly Hills, Compton, and Watts." *The Emergency Librarian* 24 (4): 8–9.

Smith, F. 1988. *Understanding Reading*. 4th ed. Hillsdale, NJ: Lawrence Erlbaum.

Smith, N. B. 1965. *American Reading Instruction: Its Development and Its Significance in Gaining a Perspective on Current Practices in Reading*. Newark, DE: International Reading Association.

Spilich, G. J., G. T. Vesonder, H. L. Chiesi, and J. F. Voss. 1979. "Test Processing in Domain-Related Information for Individuals with High and Low Domain Knowledge." *Journal of Verbal Learning and Verbal Behavior* 18: 275–290.

Stanovich, K. E. 1991. "Word Recognition: Changing Perspectives." In *Handbook of Reading Research*. Vol. 2. Eds. R. Barr, M. L. Kamil, P. Mosenthal, and P. D. Pearson. Hillsdale, NJ: Lawrence Erlbaum.

Stedman, L. C., and C. F. Kaestle. 1987. "Literacy and Reading Performance in the United States, from 1880 to the Present." *Reading Research Quarterly* 22: 8–46.

Stevens, K. C. 1982. "Can We Improve Reading by Teaching Background Information?" *Journal of Reading* 25: 326–329.

Sulzby, E. 1985. "Children's Emergent Reading of Favorite Storybooks: A Developmental Study." *Reading Research Quarterly* XX: 458–481.

Tatham, S. 1970. "Reading Comprehension of Materials Written with Select Oral Language Patterns: A Study at Grades Two and Four." *Reading Research Quarterly* V: 402–426.

Taylor, B. 1979. "Good and Poor Readers' Recall of Familiar and Unfamiliar Text." *Journal of Reading Behavior* 11: 375–388.

Teale, W. H. 1986. "Home Background and Young Children's Literacy Development." In *Emergent Literacy: Writing and Reading*. Eds. W. Teale and E. Sulzby. Norwood, NJ: Ablex.

Treiman, R. 1983. "The Structure of Spoken Syllables: Evidence from Novel Word Games." *Cognition* 15: 49–74.

———. 1985. "Onsets and Rimes as Units of Spoken Syllables: Evidence from Children." *Journal of Experimental Child Psychology* 39: 161–181.

———. 1986. "The Division Between Onsets and Rimes in English Syllables." *Journal of Memory and Language* 25: 476–491.

Treiman, R., and J. Baron. 1981. "Segmental Analysis: Development and Relation to Reading Ability." In *Reading Research: Advances in Theory and Practice*. Vol. III. Eds. G. C. MacKinnon and T. G. Waller. New York: Academic Press.

Tulving, E., and C. Gold. 1963. "Stimulus Information and Contextual Information as Determinants of Tachistoscopic Recognition of Words." *Journal of Experimental Psychology* 66: 319–327.

Tunmer, W. E., and A. R. Nesdale. 1985. "Phonemic Segmentation Skill and Beginning Reading." *Journal of Educational Psychology* 77: 417–427.

Veltema, J. 1997. "Reading Between the Lines." *California Educator*. (March).

Venezky, R. L. 1967. "English Orthography: Its Graphical Structure and Its Relation to Sound." *Reading Research Quarterly* II: 75–106.

———. 1977. "Research on Reading Processes: A Historical Perspective." *American Psychologist* 32: 339–345.

Wagstaff, J. 1996. *Phonics that Work! New Strategies for the Reading/Writing Classroom*. New York: Scholastic.

Weaver, C. 1988. *Reading Process and Practice: From Socio-Psycholinguistics to Whole Language*. Portsmouth, NH: Heinemann.

*Webster's New Collegiate Dictionary*. 1981. Springfield, MA: G. & C. Merriam Co.

Weintraub, D. M. 1997. "Schools Get Word: It's Phonics or Else." *The Orange County Register*, April 12.

Wells, G. 1985. "Preschool Literacy-Related Activities and Success in School." In *Literacy, Language, and Learning*. Eds. D. Olson, A. Hildyard, and N. Torrance. New York: Cambridge University Press.

———. 1986. *The Meaning Makers*. Portsmouth, NH: Heinemann.

White, H. 1990. "School Library Collections and Services: Ranking the States." *School Library Media Quarterly* 19 (1): 12–20.

Wood, E. R., J. Johnson, H. P. Bain, B. D. Fulton, J. B. Zharias, C. M. Achilles, M. N. Lintz, J. Folger, and C. Breda. 1990. *The State of Tennessee's Student/Teacher Achievement Ratio (STAR) Project Technical Report 1985–1990*. ERIC, ED 328356.

Wylie, R. E., and D. D. Durrell. 1970. "Teaching Vowels Through Phonograms." *Elementary English* 47: 787–791.

# Index